"There is a light that shines beyond all things on earth,

beyond the highest, the very highest heavens.

This is the light that shines in your heart."

Chandogya Upanishad

Contents

Angelicious
PLANT-BASED

Anastasia Eden

Whether you are creating it or eating it, the recipes in Angelicious are here to awaken and inspire you. Food prepared from the heart, using healthy, plant-based ingredients not only nurtures us, but also ripples far and wide. It literally makes the world a better place. This book was created to help you kindle your inner flame of compassion and inspire interconnectedness with all Life. It was born out of a desire to share delicious plant-based recipes that will keep everyone happy.

Everything is energy and this energy can either support our health or hinder it. The healthier we become, the more we find ourselves in tune with our soul, which leads us toward a more vibrant and purposeful life.

Join me in creating a plethora of soul-inspired, Angelicious cuisine and help infuse the world with Love. Let's inspire each other to become better humans. Let's move ourselves into the Light and 'be the change'. Together we can go forward and allow our deepest love to ripple out into our Sacred Earth.

Welcome to the second edition of Angelicious

Anastasia Eden

The Fundamentals of Conscious Eating
What's It All About?

In this chapter, I am going to share the essentials of conscious eating, based on my own personal journey of health and evolution. I feel blessed to have crossed paths with some leading health experts over the years, gaining invaluable insight and support for my own journey. The most humbling teacher for me however has been over 25 years of unwavering commitment to conscious eating. We each have a choice. If you feel a resonance then let's journey together into a new realm of conscious eating.

Plant-powered living

Over the last couple of decades, I've spent time with lots of people who have thrived on eating a totally plant-based diet. Doctors, business people, musicians, teachers, mothers, students and athletes of all ages, from all walks of life have consistently shown that eating a healthy diet, free from all animal products, can generate remarkable levels of health and well-being. I've seen countless people reclaim their youthfulness after having life-threatening illnesses such as crippling arthritis or cancer, by simply eating a balanced vegan diet. Fresh organic vegetables, healthy grains, seeds, nuts, beans and legumes are loaded with vitamins, minerals, phytonutrients, antioxidants, essential fats, fibre and all the protein we need for health. The important thing for wellness, is to make good quality, balanced, organic choices, free from highly processed foods. As a bonus, in an often chaotic world, this way of eating expands our capacity for compassion and can naturally help us become better humans.

My own plant-based journey from ethics to super health

Initially, for me, adopting a plant-based diet was an ethical choice. I could no longer support animal slaughter or the cruel dairy and egg industries. I've always felt that life is a gift and that it's not right to desecrate other sentient creatures. All life is sacred. A deep connection with Mother Earth from an early age, also showed me increasing evidence that animal-based diets were responsible for massive degradation of the environment. Back then, this meant destruction of vast areas of trees to grow animal fodder for the meat and dairy industries. I couldn't knowingly contribute to that. Today there is compelling evidence to show that the livestock industry is responsible for an unacceptable amount of environmental damage, including massive misuse of water (and consequent shortages), water contamination and unprecedented emissions of greenhouse gases. It has been shown to be the greatest contributor to greenhouse gas emissions, larger than all other causes put together. In addition to that, my decision to go totally plant-based was made easier when I contemplated that cows' milk was really meant for baby calves, not people. Then there was my teeth! I noticed that, as a human being, I neither had the teeth nor agility of a carnivorous animal, and, like all other humans, didn't have a digestive system that was designed to skilfully digest meat.

Within a year of going totally plant-based, the most unexpected thing was starting to happen. I was experiencing a lightness and vibrancy that I'd never had before. I felt positively alive and interconnected with sentient life. Giving up meat and animal products was freeing up lots of energy previously expended on digestion and dealing with the more harmful effects of animal products (i.e. extra cholesterol, hormones and the karma of slaughter). My body was able to naturally focus on repair and rejuvenation, so it quickly followed that I started to feel amazing. Within a year, I realised that my decision for plant-based living wasn't just a compassionate, moral choice, but I was also opting for a healthy, vibrant life too. I came alive! Since then, I have noticed the same pattern of health and vitality with others who have gone on to eat a healthy, balanced plant-based diet.

A TASTE OF AWAKENING

Beyond the mind, beyond the walls that people build to protect themselves, beyond the skin, beyond our judgements, beyond all things, there is a light, a light at the core of all sentient life. It is the essence of every living creature, every plant, every human being. This is the inspiration that helped me create this book. This is the magic that helps me create the most delicious delights in the kitchen. This is the gift I feel honoured to share with you.

Whether we realise it or not, everyone is searching for evolution, compassion, love and ever greater ways to infuse that into our lives. This book is a way to do that. Angelicious is more than just a recipe book - it's a taste of awakening, infused with compassion.

I can't save the world, but what I can do is create delicious soul-inspired recipes that infuse the world with more love and kindness. We all can. All we need do is open our hearts and create with love.

Busting the Myth on Plant-Based Protein

Plant-based protein

So where do you actually get your protein from on a plant-based diet? Interestingly, the same place that other super healthy herbivores like horses and gorillas do - plants. The secret of plant-based health is to make good protein choices by including a wide variety of vegetables, seeds, grains, nuts, pulses, beans and legumes in your diet. You can rest assured, that as long as you consume enough calories, plant foods contain plenty of protein to keep you healthy and well. Try telling a gorilla he's not getting enough protein!

Plant-based protein offers an exciting realm of healthy possibilities

When I look for answers, I realise that plant-based eating is a whole realm of its own, which can't be lumped into the usual food studies that address more conventional meat, dairy and wheat-based diets. T. Colin Campbell, author of 'The China Study,' the largest epidemiological study to date on human nutrition wrote:

> *"There is a mountain of compelling research showing that plant protein allows
> for slow but steady synthesis of new proteins,
> and is the healthiest type of protein."*

He addresses the subject in great depth in his book, using a lifetime of work and research to support his findings.

Protein and amino acids

Proteins are made up of amino acids. Each has an important function of its own within the body. Humans can manufacture some amino acids internally. Essential amino acids however, cannot be synthesised within our system and therefore must be supplied in the diet. There are 9 essential amino acids - phenylalanine, valine, threonine, tryptophan, methionine, leucine, isoleucine, lysine, and histidine. These essential amino acids are easily supplied by eating a varied and balanced plant-based diet. Several plant foods even contain all 9 essential amino acids, for example, chia seed, hempseed, buckwheat and quinoa. All other plant-based foods contain some of the essential amino acids. This means that by eating a combination of different foods over the course of your week, you will get all your requirements for these essential nutrients.

HOW MUCH PROTEIN DO WE NEED?

How much protein we need is still hotly contested. We all know that it is important. We also know that eating too much protein can lead to health issues, as the kidneys (which are responsible for metabolising protein) struggle to handle the overload. Overconsumption is frequently a problem with a diet based on animal protein (which also comes laden with saturated fats, unhealthy cholesterol and is frequently linked to cancers, heart disease and many other chronic illnesses). Plant-based protein however, comes wrapped with antioxidants, health-affirming fats, phytochemicals, vitamins and minerals which all support health rather than hinder it. Plant-based protein is essentially a win-win. I am not going to tell you exactly how much protein you need to eat - that is beyond the scope of this book. Personally speaking, I believe (and have observed in my long-term explorations) that as long as you eat a healthy, varied plant-based diet (with enough calories), then it is actually impossible not to get enough protein, because all plant-based foods contain amino acids. The key is to make sure that over the course of a week, you include some higher level protein foods in your diet, and that you vary things regularly. You'll be surprised how vibrant, strong and alive you can feel!

VARIETY IS THE KEY

Bear in mind that you will find protein in all plant foods. Variety is always best. Some of the highest protein sources include beans, lentils, peas, quinoa, grains (like buckwheat, millet and rice), nuts, seeds, and fatty fruits (like avocados and olives). Remember that protein is important for health, but including a variety of these different foods in your weekly cuisine, along with lots of fresh organic vegetables, will be more than adequate to meet your needs for healthy living. If you are very active, athletic, have extra protein requirements or just want to be extra sure you are getting enough, then you can easily add extra protein in the form of powder (such as hemp protein) to your smoothies or superfood sweet treats.

MOTHER NATURE KNOWS BEST

Mother Nature has an interesting take on protein. Human babies are designed by nature to drink human milk (not dairy milk) until they are old enough to eat solid foods. Babies are naturally meant to have rich human breast milk which contains 5% protein. Think about it, because Mother Nature knows best - this milk is designed to turn a newborn baby into a healthy, thriving toddler with the perfect amount of protein. As we grow and begin to eat solids foods, it becomes clear that by eating a healthy, herbivorous diet we get more than enough protein to meet our requirements for happy, vibrant living. In fact, it seems that it would be pretty difficult not to get enough protein, unless you eat a diet high in processed foods or have a calorie-restricted plan. I have consistently found that as long as I vary what I eat and eat good quality foods, optimal health ensues.

WORLD CLASS ATHLETES THRIVING ON PLANTS

It is helpful to know that there are many top, long-term vegan athletes who have thrived in their field, thanks to plant protein. Carl Lewis (track and field), Steph Davis (mountain climber/base jumper), Brendan Brazier (triathlete) and Fiona Oakes (record-breaking marathon runner) are just a few stars who have all excelled by eating this way.

There Are Good Fats Too You Know!

Fat has gained bad press in the mainstream over the years. However, healthy fats are important for: nervous system function, heart health, healthy hair, body fuel, hormonal support, delivery of fat-soluble vitamins (A, D, E and K), brain support, digestion, metabolism, keeping our skin soft and protecting our organs. The simple truth is that we need healthy fat.

We might be forgiven for thinking that fats are bad for us, especially after seeing the long list of chronic illnesses that are associated with diets rich in animal-based and highly processed fats. Plant-based fat (especially in its raw, unrefined form) is a completely different matter. The key words here are 'healthy fats'... and for health and longevity we need to be sure that we are making choices that help us thrive.

Did you know plant-based fat is cholesterol free?

Humans have no need for dietary cholesterol since the body naturally manufactures all that it requires from the liver. Too much cholesterol in the body is responsible for a myriad of chronic health problems. Cholesterol comes from animal-based foods such as eggs, meat and dairy products. Plant foods, on the other hand, are cholesterol-free.

The 'skinny' on essential fatty acids

Essential fatty acids are nutritional elements that human beings (and other animals) cannot manufacture themselves internally. This means we need to eat foods that contain them in order to fulfil our nutritional requirements.

There are two types of essential fats; omega-6 and omega-3. These fatty acids, which are found in plants, are crucial for the normal functioning of all tissues in the body. Plant foods provide omega-6 in the form of linoleic acid (LA) and omega-3 in the form of alpha-linoleic acid (ALA). The body converts these into various compounds that are responsible for healthy human existence.

Omega-6 is generally over consumed by a long way (even on plant-based diets); whereas omega-3 tends to be under consumed. In most conventional diets (and even lots of well meaning plant-based diets) people often consume these fatty acids at an omega-6 to omega-3 ratio of anything between 10:1 and 25:1. This is out of balance. For optimal health, the balance is thought to be between 2:1 to 4:1 (omega 6: omega-3). Eating too much omega-6 can actually inhibit the action of omega-3, so it's important to work on getting the balance right with adequate daily amounts of omega-3 fatty acids (you are probably already well covered on the omega-6 front). Good sources of omega-3 include flaxseeds, hempseeds, chia seeds, walnuts and some leafy vegetables and beans.

The best way to get your healthy fats

The best way to incorporate healthy fats into your diet is to make sure you include a variety of nuts and seeds (which also come in the form of nut and seed butters) and fatty fruits like avocado, olives or coconut. If you use oil for dressing salads then this can also be a great source of essential fatty acid nutrition, especially if you use a good quality, organic, cold-pressed or extra virgin oil. I favour hempseed oil and flaxseed oil (which should not be heated).

Flaxseeds: The omega-3 super star

Flaxseed oil and ground flaxseeds are excellent options to support your requirements for omega-3 fatty acids. There isn't an official dosage, although it is thought that one teaspoon of flaxseed oil or one to two tablespoons of ground flaxseed will give you the recommended daily requirement of ALA (alpha-linoleic acid). I would say that this is a minimum figure. Flaxseeds are difficult to digest whole, so be sure to grind them into a meal before eating, to gain maximum benefit. You can also purchase them pre-ground. It is best to store them in the fridge or freezer to reduce the effects of potential oxygen damage. And whilst my favourite way to enjoy ground flaxseeds is raw, it's also fine to heat them (great for baking), since, in studies, the seeds have clearly been shown to remain stable when baked. Flaxseed oil is however unstable when heated, which can load it with free radicals (bad news for health), so it's important that you don't heat these oils.

Hempseeds: Perfectly balanced for omega-6 and omega-3

My personal favourite oil for salad dressings is cold-pressed hempseed oil. It contains an ideal omega-6 to omega-3 ratio of 3:1. As with flaxseed oil, always buy a good quality oil and be sure never to heat it. Hulled hempseeds also make a great salad or breakfast sprinkle. You can find out more about this super healthy seed on page 57.

Coconut oil is best for cooking

Heating most oils generally makes them unstable, creating free radicals, which can in turn wreak havoc in the body. For this reason, I recommend you get your daily essential fatty acids from raw, unprocessed wholefoods (like nuts, seeds and avocados) or cold-pressed oils (in moderation). There are times however, when we might want to do a quick sauté, bake a cake or whip up some granola. In this case, the best known oil for cooking is coconut oil. It has been shown to remain stable and healthier for a much longer period during heating than other oils. So for cooking, coconut oil comes up top and is a good choice for cooked and baked goods. The stability of other oils is debatable and research is coming up with new data all the time. My feeling is that a little dash of oil for cooking here and there is not going to hurt.

Gluten-Free - A Growing Movement

Gluten has been scientifically proven to contribute to most chronic diseases. The research on the effects of gluten from peer-reviewed medical journals in recent years is plentiful. Gluten has even been shown to be a major contributing factor in some mental health issues such as schizophrenia and depression.

I had eaten a wheat-free, low gluten diet for most of my adult life, enjoying grains such as spelt, barley and rye from time to time (which have a lower gluten content than wheat). Balanced with a nutrient-dense plant food diet, free from refined sugar, minimising gluten can be an excellent way to support health. If you aren't sensitive to gluten then you might find lower gluten grains better for health.

A good few years back, I began to experience brain fog, tiredness, lack of energy and occasional stomach cramps which seemed to coincide with eating gluten foods. Even though my diet was healthy, full of nutrients, free from refined sugar and animal products, I realised that the one thing that was possibly still compromising my health was gluten. I did an experiment, eliminated gluten from my diet and felt better and have kept it at bay ever since.

Gluten taking its toll

Recent years have seen a phenomenal rise in people with gluten sensitivity, intolerance or allergy. Some people are finding that if they cut gluten out of their diet (or significantly reduce it), they feel so much better, seeing improvement in health levels.

Going gluten-free or reducing gluten intake is easy if you are prepared to get creative and learn new dishes in the kitchen. This book has lots of great ideas for going gluten-free. Culinary adventures await! If you want to eat out then you'll be pleased to know that it's common to find restaurants catering for the rapidly expanding 'free-from' population.

Giving up gluten elevated my energy by a quantum leap. I must admit that I did, however, go into a momentary panic as I felt my 'occasional chunk of spelt bread dunked in soup' and my British 'beans on toast' bite the dust. I had to stay open-minded and trust that those things would be replaced with new alternatives. It is so often the case when we are on the path of health, that when we think we have to 'give something up', we are not losing out at all, but reclaiming an aspect of ourselves in the process.

Even though I didn't eat a lot of gluten, it was beginning to take its toll, having a cumulative effect on my system. Within a short period of eliminating it completely, my health felt incredible once again. I have only had gluten again accidentally no more than a handful of times. On those occasions I was temporarily doubled over with stomach cramp hours after consuming it. The innate intelligence of our body is incredible if we give it the space to guide us. The secret of health is to listen.

CAN THIS MANY PEOPLE BE WRONG?

I have lost count of the people who have independently approached me and said that they felt much clearer and healthier after giving up gluten. These aren't always people with diagnosed illness either. They are often regular people who just give it a go. They might also be people who already care about their health and are in-tune enough to recognise that their body is guiding them towards better choices. These people have often seen the difference in energy levels and gut health when they omit gluten from their diet.

TAKING RESPONSIBILITY FOR OUR OWN CHOICES

Some people can get away with eating more gluten than others, although I am sure that everyone would benefit from a low gluten or gluten-free diet. Whether we are ill or not, we have the power to take responsibility for our own health. We don't need to wait until we get a chronic illness or feel so depressed that we can't bear to go on any longer; if we have reached that point, then we have to do so much more work to repair the damage that has been slowly chipping away at us for years. Prevention is the best cure.

WORLD CLASS ATHLETES GOING GLUTEN-FREE

The major problem is that gluten is tough for our digestive system to break down; we end up expending a lot of energy just to get it through our system. Nowadays, it is common to find that top athletes have gone gluten-free during competitions, because they have observed that their athletic recovery rates are much faster without this glue-like substance. For the rest of us, eliminating or reducing gluten over time (along with a balanced, plant-based diet) can free up energy, preventing premature ageing and chronic diseases that follow a continually compromised system.

SENSITIVITY IS OUR SAVING GRACE

Sensitivity (whether to gluten or any foods) is an intelligent response to food substances that are unhealthy and not generally suited for human consumption. Sensitivity is bit like an inbuilt early warning system. People often say, 'but it doesn't affect me'. They seem immune to the effects of unhealthy foods. This may actually be a disadvantage, because some people may experience an unnoticed, slow degradation of health, that accumulates over time, not fully rearing its ugly head until it manifests as a life-threatening illness, by which point it is often too late. Let natural sensitivity guide you and learn to listen to your body.

Wheat is the worst culprit

Modern day wheat has a lot to answer for in the midst of the current gluten intolerance epidemic. Wheat has been hybridised for the high-yielding commercial market and is a world apart from its ancient cousins (such as spelt or kamut). Not only is wheat remarkably high in gluten, it also contains other components such as wheat germ agglutinin (WGA), a lectin, which has been shown to impede physical and mental wellbeing. WGA is a neurotoxin (a neurotoxin is a poison that acts on the nervous system) that crosses the blood-brain barrier, attaches to the myelin sheath, and can inhibit nerve growth and action. This has implications for degenerative neurological disorders like multiple sclerosis, Alzheimer's and issues such as depression, schizophrenia and bipolar disorder. These are some of the known problems with conventional and organic wheat; just imagine what a cocktail of issues opens up when you include the recent addition of genetically modified organisms into that equation!

Coeliac disease - gluten turns aggressive

This is the most severe form of sensitivity to gluten. Coeliac disease is an auto-immune response to the gluten protein found in grains such as wheat, spelt, barley and rye. It is characterised by gastrointestinal disorders and the inability to absorb nutrients from food due to damaged villi in the small intestine. In these cases, people really have absolutely no choice but to eliminate gluten from the diet, since that is the only known treatment. Instances of coeliac disease have sky-rocketed in recent years and continue on a steady curve upwards.

Whatever your reasons

Whether you are allergic or intolerant to gluten, have coeliac disease or you just want to make smart health choices, there are a plethora of different recipes in this book to support your journey to health. Every recipe is packed with nutritional goodness to nourish you and help you establish a healthy way of eating for life.

As the old, unhealthy ways steadily drop from your diet, you'll be amazed at what a difference such changes can make. Get ready to rocket!

Vitamin B12 - The Hot Debate

Vitamin B12 is crucial for the formation of red blood cells, as well as for the proper functioning and health of nerve tissue. This important vitamin is a hot subject of discussion in the plant-based food world, because it happens to be the only nutrient we can't get from plants. This is pretty much due to our western habit of thoroughly cleaning everything. Not only do we clean away the bad stuff, we also clean away things that may actually be beneficial for us. You see, B12 is made by micro-organisms. Other (non-human) herbivorous (plant-eating) animals obtain B12 from bacteria within the digestive system as a completely natural process. Until our world became so clinical and rigorous with food washing and anti-bacterial practices, we humans would have naturally ingested it on the micro-organisms from foraged or garden grown foods. Since our world became so keen on anti-bacterial cleansing, the healthy, natural gut flora of human beings has been pretty much decimated, meaning that the only sure way to obtain B12 on a plant-based diet is to supplement regularly... that is unless of course we return to nature and go back to the wild. Deficiency of this nutrient can be serious, so I strongly suggest that you regularly supplement with a good quality source of B12. The body is known to store B12 for a long period of time, so if you miss it out from time to time, you will probably be fine. However, do make sure that you top up regularly. B12 supplements are available in any good health food store and the best quality brands usually give you a really high dosage.

You Are Amazing!

Having said all that, it's important to remember that the most crucial thing about eating consciously is that you enjoy your food. Positivity and joy are as equally responsible for good health and longevity as nutritional content. So, whatever you do, embrace the moment, let go of any stress and allow your life to become the most beautiful expression of the amazing soul that you are. Because you ARE amazing. Let that light shine forth!

Morning Time & Breakfast

Sunrise Fruit Bowls

Fruit is a great way to start the day. It helps to ease your digestive system back into gear after a night of 'fasting'. In an ideal world we would just eat a piece of fruit exactly the way it comes, straight off the tree without anything added, just as nature intended. However, our modern lifestyles often call out for a few little extra things to help us deal with the intensity of busy lives. At other times, we might just want to make things a little more exciting and colourful.

The seasons bring lots of different fruits, so use whatever fruits you have available to you. Be sure to use organic or unsprayed produce. The most exciting time for fruits here in Britain is late spring until late autumn, where you find gardens adorned with berries, blueberries, plums, cherries, currants and later on wild blackberries, apples and pears. Here's a great way to enjoy fruit for breakfast - with fruit, sauce and topping ideas listed opposite.

1. Choose and chop fruit.
2. Choose a sauce to drizzle on top or mix in.
3. Add a topping. Sprinkle a small handful on top or mix in as desired and savour the moment.

Fruit ideas

- mango
- apple
- banana
- strawberries
- raspberries
- blueberries
- blackberries
- cherimoya
- papaya
- figs
- plums
- cherries
- pear
- peaches
- apricots
- pineapple
- kiwi fruits

Sauce ideas

Coconut yoghurt: just add a generous dollop

Plant-based yoghurt: use your favourite sugar-free, dairy-free yoghurt

Coconut cream with a sprinkle of coconut sugar: mix a tablespoon with your fruit

Tahini: mix a spoonful of tahini with a little plant milk in a small bowl until it resembles a cream

Orange juice: a splash of freshly squeezed to create a fruit salad

No sauce: perfect if you are in a hurry

Topping ideas

Soft nuts: walnuts, pecans and cashews

Hard nuts: brazils, hazelnuts and almonds

Seeds (whole or ground): sunflower, pumpkin, chia, flax, sesame

Dried fruits: raisins, dates, figs, apricots, goji berries

Coconut: shredded, desiccated or flaked

Sprinkle of superfoods: powdered maca, barley grass powder, cacao nibs

Granola: try 'Crunchy Buckwheat Almond Granola' (see page 24)

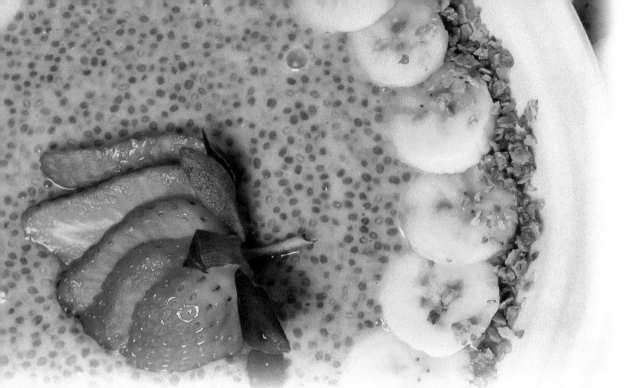

Strawberry Chia Breakfast Bowl

Serves: *1*

Time: *5 mins*
(plus over night soaking)

Ingredients:
250ml plant-based milk
1 teaspoon vanilla extract
3 large organic strawberries
1 tablespoon of coconut cream
3 tablespoons chia seeds
Fresh fruit to garnish (optional)
A sprinkle of gluten-free granola
(optional)

This is an excellent breakfast to prepare if you want a super healthy start to the day. The preparation is quick, easy and happens the night before, making it an ideal dish if you are rushed in the mornings, yet don't want to compromise on nutrition. Chia seeds are tiny, nutrient-rich and loaded with proteins, antioxidants, omega-3 fatty acids, vitamins, minerals and phytonutrients. They are an excellent source of calcium, phosphorus and magnesium, all of which are beneficial for bone health. Soaking the chia seeds over night turns them into a thick, scrumptious, gel-like pudding. Add in a few extras and you have a delicious breakfast bowl.

1. Blend the plant-based milk, vanilla extract, strawberries and coconut cream to create a strawberry 'milk'.
2. Stir the whole chia seeds into the strawberry milk that you've just made and pop into the fridge.
3. Go back and stir it again after about a half hour (this stops the chia seeds from all sticking together). Pop it back into the fridge and leave over night.
4. Give it a stir the next morning and serve with a generous sprinkle of fresh fruits and/or gluten-free granola.

ABOUT CHIA SEEDS

Chia seeds are one of the richest plant-based sources of essential fats, a high quality protein food and are loaded with antioxidants. They are little seeds that form a gel when soaked in water. You'll find they work well in smoothies, ground down and added to salads or with breakfast as a sprinkle.

CRUNCHY BUCKWHEAT ALMOND GRANOLA

Buckwheat flakes make a great alternative to rolled oats. Even though it is generally sold as a grain, buckwheat is in fact a seed related to the rhubarb and sorrel family. Naturally gluten-free, it's a great protein food containing all of the essential amino acids. Buckwheat is also particularly high in flavonoids, which help to protect us against disease. This recipe makes a gorgeous, crunchy cereal that serves well with plant-based milk or as a crispy textured topping on a smoothie bowl. It also benefits from ground flaxseeds, which are loaded with healthy essential fats and antioxidants. Whilst it isn't recommend that flaxseed oil is used in baking, research shows that the omega-3 fats and phytonutrients in flaxseeds are remarkably heat stable, making them a perfect addition to this super healthy granola. Use less oil if you prefer less crunch.

Serves: 4 - 6

Time: 35 mins

Ingredients:

100ml coconut oil

50g blanched almonds

250g buckwheat flakes

4 tablespoons ground almonds

2 tablespoons ground flaxseeds

75ml maple syrup or brown rice syrup

1 teaspoon almond essence

1. If your coconut oil is solid then melt it ahead of time by putting in a warm place. It needs to be liquid so that you can measure it and then mix it in.
2. Preheat oven to gas mark 4 (350°F/180°C).
3. Roughly chop the blanched almonds into halves or quarters.
4. Add all ingredients to a mixing bowl and then mix until everything is well coated with the oil and syrup. If your container or kitchen is a little chilly then the coconut oil may start to solidify in the mixing process, in which case it is much easier to use your hands to mix by repeatedly rubbing in with your fingers.
5. Place on a baking tray approximately 30 x 25cm (12 x 10inches) and compact down firmly.
6. Pop into the preheated oven and bake for about 20 minutes before breaking it up, stirring in and then pressing down firmly again. Pop back into the oven and bake for another 10 minutes (or until lightly tanned on top).
7. When ready, take out of the oven and allow to cool down before breaking up into granola pieces.

Seeds of Life Granola

Here's a delicious granola seed recipe using oats and a variety of health-affirming seeds. If you eat exclusively gluten-free, then be extra sure to purchase certified 'gluten-free' oats.

1. Melt your coconut oil by placing it in a warm place (such as a sunny window sill or above a radiator) ahead of time.
2. Preheat the oven to gas mark 5 (190°C/375°F).
3. Mix all the dry ingredients together in a mixing bowl (if your sesame and flaxseeds aren't already ground, use a nut mill or high-powered food processor/blender to grind them to a meal).
4. Mix in the coconut oil, brown rice syrup and vanilla essence thoroughly. If your kitchen is a little cold, then the coconut oil may start to solidify before you have finished, making it a little harder to coat the granola. If this is the case, then mix and rub in with your hands instead (it's more fun that way and the warmth of your hands will soften the coconut oil).
5. Once evenly coated, place the mixture onto a large baking tray, pressing it down firmly with either your hands or the back of a spoon. It should all stick together, forming a solid mass.
6. Pop the tray in the oven. After about 15 minutes (or when it starts to lightly tan) take it out and then break up the mixture. Press back down firmly with a spoon and then pop back in the oven for another 10 minutes. It should be lightly tanned by this time.
7. When the cooking time is over, take out of the oven and allow to fully cool down.
8. Once cool, take a blunt knife and spoon to prise up the granola (which should still be one solid mass) breaking it into chunks. If some of the chunks are too big, then break them down a little more.
9. Serve with your favourite plant-based milk along with freshly chopped or dried fruit.

Serves: *4 - 6*

Time: *30 mins*

Ingredients:
100ml coconut oil
250g rolled oats
3 tablespoons sunflower seeds
2 tablespoons pumpkin seeds
2 tablespoons ground flaxseeds
50g ground sesame seeds
1 tablespoon cinnamon
2 teaspoon vanilla
¼ teaspoon ground ginger
75ml brown rice syrup
(or alternative)
2 teaspoon vanilla extract

WINTER MILLET ALMOND PORRIDGE

Serves: *2*

Time: *35 mins*
(plus extra optional 'sitting' time)

Ingredients:
100g whole millet
400ml plant milk
7 dates or 2 tablespoons raisins
40g blanched almonds
½ teaspoon almond essence
1 small banana
Extra water or plant milk
4 tablespoons of coconut cream or coconut yoghurt
A generous dollop of sugar-free fruit spread/jam (optional)

When the winter sets in and those cold days start grinding you down, this is an excellent morning meal that will keep you feeling satiated and nourished all the way through to lunchtime. Millet is an ancient, gluten-free seed used just like a grain. It is often cooked like rice, quinoa or oats and comes either whole, ground or in flakes. Not only is the millet in this dish alkalising, it has also been found to contain serotonin, which can help to stabilise your mood and alleviate the winter blues. In this recipe I'm using whole millet and almonds to create a filling, nutritious porridge.

1. Put the millet and rice milk into a sauce pan and add the raisins, almonds, almond essence and banana.
2. Bring to the boil and then reduce to a light simmer. Place lid on to the pan.
3. Allow to cook for about 35 minutes, stirring every once in a while.
4. If the plant milk boils off or absorbs too rapidly, add extra as required.
5. Add up to 4 tablespoons of coconut cream or coconut yoghurt and mix in a minute or two before you take off the heat.
6. Once cooked you can serve straight away. Better still, if you have the time, leave it with the heat turned off for between ten minutes and a half an hour before you eat. This gives the ingredients extra time to dance together and works a treat.
7. If you like, add a generous dollop of sugar-free fruit spread or jam before you eat.

millet grains

HOT QUINOA BREAKFAST BOWL

When deciding on what to eat for breakfast, I want to make sure that every morsel is healthful, nutritious and of course, delicious. This is where my 'Quinoa Breakfast Bowl' works a treat. It's the perfect, cooked, gluten-free, dairy-free morning meal. This dish leaves me feeling vibrant, light and alive as well as pleasantly nourished and satiated. It's ideal for occasions where regular oat porridge would be just too heavy. Use fair trade organic quinoa and a good quality organic, canned coconut milk for the best results.

1. Rinse quinoa thoroughly using an extra fine sieve. This removes any of the natural soapy saponins that sometimes coat quinoa.
2. Chop dates into small pieces and then add all ingredients (apart from the cinnamon or berries - which will be added once served) to a pan.
3. Bring pan to the boil and simmer on a low heat for 25 minutes (or until the quinoa has absorbed all of the liquid). Stir once in a while with a wooden spoon. The dates should slowly fall apart, melting into the pan to create a delicious sweetness. If the dates are particularly tough, encourage the breaking down process by pressing them down with your spoon.
4. Once cooked, enjoy your quinoa bowl served hot or cold, adding a sprinkle of cinnamon and/or a small handful of fresh berries.

Serves: *1*

Time: *25 mins*

Ingredients:
50g quinoa
5 pitted dates
200ml canned coconut milk
50ml water
Sprinkle of cinnamon (optional)
Fresh berries (optional)

Green Hemp Protein Smoothie

Hemp truly is a superfood. Not only is it full of minerals and vitamins, it contains all 21 amino acids that humans are known to use (including the 9 essential amino acids that the human body can't make itself and therefore must acquire from food). Hemp is said to be one of the most powerful sources of protein in the plant kingdom. It also brings a fine offering of essential fatty acids containing nature's perfect balance of omega-3 and omega-6. Most other seeds offer little in the way of omega-3, so hemp is a real gift. Hemp smoothies are one of the ways that I have found to keep this super seed showing up in my weekly diet. My recipe here is an excellent, light way to get your day off to a good start with a nourishing blend of hemp, greens, lemon and fruits.

Serves: *1 glass*

Time: *5 mins*

Ingredients:

1 lemon
1 large apple
1 banana
1 large kale leaf
2 to 3 tablespoons hempseeds
5 ice cubes
(made with filtered or spring water)
Water (filtered or spring)

1. Squeeze the lemon and discard the peel.
2. Chop the apple into small chunks. You can leave the skin on but discard the core.
3. Add all ingredients into your blending jug, adding the ice cubes last.
4. Pour in approximately 150ml of pure spring (or filtered) water and then blend, adding a little more water if required.
5. Keep blending until you reach your preferred smoothie consistency.
6. For optimal vibrancy, enjoy immediately.

Blueberry & Lemon Cosmic Smoothie

Serves: *1 glass*

Time: *5 mins*

Ingredients:

50g cashews (soaked)
1 large chopped frozen banana
100g of frozen blueberries
1 small lemon (juiced)
250ml (1 cup) almond milk
Dash of vanilla extract

All ingredients in this smoothie are designed by nature to support your health. Not only is it lip-lickin' delicious, it also has a welcomed immune supporting ability. Like most sweet berries, blueberries are full of antioxidants. Lemon helps to bring out the best in all of the other flavours, whilst working its natural medicinal magic, loaded with vitamin C and acting as a powerful anti-viral, anti-bacterial and antioxidant. Cashews add a little *je ne sais quoi*, bringing in a welcomed depth. Their essential fatty acids help slow down the release of the natural fruit sugar from the fruits - which can help keep us energised and satiated for longer.

It's not actually essential to soak the cashews in advance, although, if you do have the time (and remember), then soaking them and draining for at least an hour beforehand (or even overnight) makes them luxuriously soft and blend-able (especially handy if you don't have a high-powered blender). If you miss this soaking part out, the unsoaked cashews can make the smoothie ever so slightly bitty and rustic (which can be very nice too).

1. If you are using the soaked cashew method then be sure to put them in some water ahead of time (at least an hour), then rinse and drain before blending.
2. Add all ingredients to your blender and blend until you achieve your desired consistency.
3. Add a little extra almond milk if you want to thin it down.
4. Enjoy.

Mango – "The King of Fruits"

Mango is one of the most popular fruits in the world, commonly known as 'the King of Fruits'. You'll find it far and wide, thriving in frost-free tropical and sub-tropical regions across the globe. The mango is thought to have originated in India, where to this very day it is the national fruit, having a huge cultural significance in worshipping certain deities, blessing births, honouring weddings and other celebrations.

Apart from its lusciously sweet, tropical flavour and heaven-sent fragrance, the mango delivers quite a plethora of nutrients. 100g of mango is said to deliver a massive 100% of the recommended daily allowance of vitamin C. Mango has also been shown to have high levels of vitamin A, folate, antioxidants and good levels of various minerals such as copper and potassium. Mango is host to many hidden qualities that support health, most of which have been tried and tested in ethnic communities for centuries.

One of the best ways to enjoy a mango is by scooping it right out of the skin and eating on its own. In fact, most of the mangoes I eat are gone before they even make it into a smoothie! That said, they do, however, make an excellent addition to a smoothie. Mangoes can help to create a creamy, flavoursome, aromatic experience that - if you get a really good mango - is second to none.

How to prepare a mango:

A ripe mango will 'give' slightly when you press it. It is easiest to slice down either side of the pit with a sharp knife, score it into cubes and then press up from the underside to expose an exciting hedgehog-like fan of mango cubes. These are easily eaten right off the skin or scooped out with a metal spoon.

Mango Superfood Smoothies

Sweet Berry & Almond Mango Smoothie

Almonds are a great source of nutrients, plentiful in minerals and B and E vitamins.

Small handful of almonds
2 dates
1 small mango
200g frozen strawberries or raspberries
200ml water

1. Soak almonds and dates overnight to make them soft and easier to blend. Strain off the water and rinse the almonds before placing in your blender.
2. Dice the mango.
3. Blend all ingredients in a blender until you reach a smooth, creamy consistency.

Malty Maca Mango Smoothie

Maca is a powerful smoothie addition, best known for its malty taste and hormone balancing properties.

½ large mango
1 ripe banana
150ml plant-based milk
1 tablespoon maca powder
1 tablespoon coconut cream
1 heaped tablespoon desiccated coconut (optional)

1. Peel and dice fruit then blend all ingredients.
2. Garnish with sprinkle of desiccated coconut.

Blackberry & Mango Smoothie

For optimal antioxidant benefits, black-berries are best foraged in wild hedge-rows in season. Frozen blackberries work well too.

½ ripe medium/large mango
Handful of ripe blackberries
200ml plant-based milk (or water)
1 tablespoon of tahini

1. Dice mango and then blend all ingredients together until you find a smooth, creamy consistency.

Creamy Garden Berry Smoothie

There's something deeply satisfying about the vibrant sweetness of a summer garden berry smoothie, especially with fruit freshly gathered from your own raspberry and strawberry plants (if you are fortunate enough to grow your own). During berry season, I enjoy a tasty smoothie most mornings for breakfast. It also works wonders as a refreshing afternoon treat.

Berries are packed with all sorts of nutritional benefits like vitamin C and antioxidants. They are brimming with health affirming goodness. Heaven only knows how they get to taste so incredibly delicious. In this recipe, the frozen banana is the secret *je ne sais quoi* that delivers the thick creaminess.

Serves: *1 glass*

Time: *5 mins*
(plus time to freeze)

Ingredients:
1 large banana (frozen in chunks)
*Large handful of strawberries
and raspberries*
200ml rice or coconut milk

1. The first step is to freeze the banana in advance. This is a great way to use up ripe bananas as they'll store in the freezer for a few months. The best way to freeze them for smoothie making is to peel off the skin and then chop into chunks. Put the chunks into a container and then pop them into the freezer. Give your banana at least a few hours to freeze (you really do need to plan ahead with this part - although you'll be glad that you did).
2. Take the chopped banana out of the freezer and place into a blending jug along with the berries and rice milk. Use less milk if you want a super thick smoothie; use a little more if you want it to be more like a milkshake. Blend all ingredients together until you achieve a thick creamy consistency.
3. Pour into a glass and take some time to really enjoy the vibrant energy of your smoothie. You've gone to the effort of making it, so be sure to sit back and savour the delicious taste. Some people enjoy this with a spoon or a straw. I generally just sip straight from the glass. It works well as a smoothie bowl too, sprinkled with fresh fruits or granola.

Moringa Superfood Smoothie

Serves: *1 glass*

Time: *5 mins*

Ingredients:

200ml plant-based milk
1 large banana
60g frozen blueberries
60g fresh raspberries
1 heaped teaspoon moringa powder
1 heaped teaspoon ground flaxseed
1 heaped teaspoon maca powder
1 heaped teaspoon tahini

I started making up this particular blend to give myself a super infusion of nutrition. It's one of my favourite smoothies, containing some of the healthiest and nutritious plant-based foods on our planet.

Take for example moringa powder. It is said to contain an impressive 46 different antioxidants, 18 amino acids (including all 9 essential amino acids), 10 times the vitamin A of carrots, 15 times the potassium of bananas, 17 times the calcium of cows milk and 25 times the iron of spinach. Moringa is also an antioxidant superstar, helps to reduce blood pressure, supports liver and eye health, and is a good anti-inflammatory.

Then there's maca, an incredible plant, growing at extremely high altitudes (7000ft and above) in the Peruvian Mountains. It has adaptogenic properties (an adaptogen helps you cope in stressful situations). Maca is well known for supporting and regulating the endocrine (hormone) system in both men and women. Healthy hormones are essential for regulation of energy levels, digestion, brain function, the nervous system, fertility and wellness in general.

Flaxseeds bring in a super dose of lignans and omega-3... (check out page 135 for more about flax).

Blueberries and raspberries are 'super' fruits, full of antioxidants, vitamin C and beneficial phytonutrients. These nutrients have been shown to help support health, protect against cancer and heart disease whilst having a massive list of health affirming goodness; an excellent choice for a superfood smoothie (not to mention that gorgeous colour!).

The combination of all the ingredients in this smoothie make it deliciously nutritious.

1. Place all ingredients together in a jug for blending.
2. Blend until creamy smooth.
3. Sprinkle with extra ground fresh berries (optional).
4. Best served immediately.

Super Healthy Salads

'Eat Your Greens' Avocado Cream Salad

Serves: 4

Time: *10 mins*

Salad ingredients:
1 small broccoli head
4 large kale leaves
5 large celery stalks
1 sweet bell pepper

Sauce ingredients:
An inch cubed fresh ginger
1 clove garlic
1 medium/large ripe avocado
1 tablespoon tamari
1 tablespoon apple cider vinegar
Small handful of fresh parsley

Every morsel of this salad is power packed with with vitamins, minerals, essential fats and nutrients to support clean, healthy living. As well as an admirable array of nutrients, the raw ginger, garlic and parsley are perfectly suited to give your immune system an extra boost. This is a tasty, creative way to keep you coming back for nutrient-dense salads.

1. Chop broccoli and kale into very small pieces - as fine as you can with a sharp knife. If you have a food processor, you might even like to give it a whirl in there; that will chop it down finely in no time.
2. Chop the celery stalks and bell pepper (de-seeded), then toss them into a large salad bowl along with the finely chopped broccoli and kale.

Make the sauce as follows:
1. Peel and finely grate the ginger.
2. Smash and finely chop the garlic.
3. Scoop out the avocado flesh and either mash with a fork or potato masher or place in a blending jug. Mash or blend along with the grated ginger, garlic, tamari, apple cider vinegar and parsley.
4. Mix the sauce into the vegetables and serve.

Beet-It Ginger Salad

Hailed as a superfood, the humble beetroot (also known as beet) is a little treasure trove of health-affirming goodness. Not only is it rich in essential nutrients and works as a powerful antioxidant, it has also been shown to help lower blood pressure whilst helping your energy levels. It is definitely one of my top foods. Each ingredient, from the freshly grated ginger to the toasted sesame oil, plays an important role in making this salad so tasty.

1. Scrub beetroot and sweet potato, then grate into a mixing bowl. Leave the skins on for extra goodness (unless they are not organic).
2. Grate ginger with a fine grater (removing skin before you grate).
3. Mash avocado with a fork in a separate bowl.
4. Juice lemon and discard the skin.
5. Chop pepper into small squares.
6. Put all ingredients into a salad bowl together and mix thoroughly, until everything is evenly coated throughout.

Serves: *2*

Time: *10 mins*

Ingredients:

1 large raw beetroot
1 small sweet potato
1 heaped teaspoon grated ginger
1 ripe avocado
1 large lemon (juiced)
1 red sweet pepper
Large pinch sea salt
1 teaspoon caraway seed
1 teaspoon toasted sesame oil
Small handful of fresh parsley

The 'Look After Yourself' Kale Wrap

Serves: *1*

Time: *5 mins*

Ingredients:

½ large ripe avocado
½ lemon (juiced)
1 large garlic clove
A packed handful of parsley
1 small beetroot (raw)
½ a bell pepper
4 cherry tomatoes
1 or 2 really large kale leaves

When the body is under stress nutrients burn up rapidly. At these times I am often guided to start drinking more fresh vegetable juices for an almost immediate infusion of nutrition. My body also usually invites me to eat super healthy, raw foods, with herbs like parsley and coriander leaves or roots like ginger, garlic and turmeric. This kale wrap in the photo is exactly the sort of thing that I might have to give me a super boost (although, not forgetting that it makes an excellent every day salad too). It's a power house of nutrition, full of essential fats, vitamins, minerals and antioxidants with a strong infusion of garlic to really cleanse and enhance efficiency of the immune system.

1. Scoop out the avocado flesh and blend in a jug with the lemon juice, garlic & parsley - using a hand blender.
2. Scrub and grate your beetroot.
3. Slice bell pepper and tomatoes.
4. Stretch out your kale leaves and fill with the avocado mix, beetroot and tomatoes, wrapping tightly before eating, just like a burrito wrap.

VITALITY SALAD
WITH ALMOND BUTTER DRESSING

I must admit, there was a time I really didn't know what to do with beetroot. I'd pass it by at the farmers' market every week wondering what on earth people got so excited about. Then one day, I decided that no matter what, I was going to really make the effort and see what culinary delights wanted to happen. I ordered a big box from my local wholesaler (because I don't do things in halves), tried all sorts - grating, baking, steaming and blending - and have since created some mouthwatering dishes as a result.

In this recipe I am sharing a simple, super healthful salad recipe, because you can never eat too many healthy salads. This is the sort of thing I eat regularly for lunch. It serves well as a side dish with rice, potato wedges, millet or quinoa, or as part of a salad buffet medley along with a delicious dip. Everything about this salad is health-affirming.

1. Peel and finely grate the ginger, then add to a jug along with all the other 'sauce ingredients'. Mix together with a spoon until you reach a blended consistency.
2. Grate the beetroot and carrot.
3. Finely chop the cabbage.
4. Chop the apple (with skin still on) into small cubes.
5. Add sauce to the grated carrot & beetroot and chopped apple & cabbage - then toss together in a large salad bowl.
6. Finally, roughly chop the coriander leaves and mix in.
7. Serve fresh and enjoy.

Serves: *2*

Time: *10 mins*

Sauce ingredients:
1 teaspoon grated ginger
1 heaped tablespoon almond butter
1 tablespoon hemp oil
1 lemon (juiced)
1 teaspoon toasted sesame oil
½ teaspoon celtic sea salt
1 teaspoon tamari
1 teaspoon apple cider vinegar

Salad ingredients:
1 large carrot
1 large raw beetroot
Handful of white cabbage
1 small apple (with skin)
Handful of coriander leaves

Raw Cauliflower Salad
WITH NUTMEG & TAHINI SAUCE

Serves: 4

Time: *10 mins*

Ingredients:

1 small cauliflower
½ red sweet bell pepper
A large kale leaf
Sprinkle of hulled hempseeds or cashew nuts (optional)

Sauce ingredients:

3 heaped tablespoons tahini
1 tablespoon apple cider vinegar
2 tablespoons water (approx)
½ teaspoon freshly grated nutmeg
½ to 1 teaspoon finely grated ginger
¼ teaspoon celtic sea salt

Raw cauliflower really comes into its element with a creamy tahini dressing. The extra addition of ginger and nutmeg make this a lovely warming, nurturing dish. It serves well as part of a salad buffet or with rice, quinoa or millet.

1. Chop the cauliflower into small pieces.
2. Chop the pepper and kale into small pieces.
3. Create the sauce by mixing the tahini and apple cider vinegar together with a spoon and slowly adding the water until you get a creamy consistency. The consistency will depend on the original thickness of the tahini (which varies from jar to jar and brand to brand). If you need more liquid, just add a little more water and mix. Add the freshly grated nutmeg, finely grated ginger and sea salt.
4. Mix the sauce into the cauliflower salad.
5. Serve cold or at room temperature and enjoy.

Serves: *2*

Time: *15 mins*

Ingredients:
1 large lemon
4 kale leaves
Big pinch of freshly grated nutmeg
Pinch of celtic sea salt (to taste)
1 carrot
3 celery sticks
1 small ripe avocado
2 tablespoons of nuts or seeds

GRILLED LEMON
KALE MASSAGE SALAD

Grilling magically transforms the flavour of lemon, bringing down the sharp tones and imbuing a deep warming flavour. And yes, you really do massage your kale in this recipe! This not only infuses the freshly grilled lemon into the kale, it also softens it for easier chewing. The nutmeg gently complements the lemon, creating a culinary feast of deliciousness.

1. Slice and grill your lemon under a medium grill until you start to see the tops browning a little.
2. Whilst you are waiting for the lemon to grill, prepare your veggies.
3. De-stalk and finely chop your kale into small pieces. Toss into your bowl along with the freshly grated nutmeg and sea salt.
4. Chop your carrot and celery into super small pieces and put to the side (don't add to the kale yet - the kale needs to be massaged with the lemon first).
5. Dice your avocado and leave on the side too.
6. Once the lemon is grilled, use a sieve to squeeze out all of the juice directly onto the kale before massaging in with you hands for a couple of minutes. When you are satisfied that all of the kale has been coated, then toss in your carrots, celery and avocado.
7. Sprinkle with nuts or seeds of your choosing (I like sunflower or pumpkin seeds) and then serve.

Raw Pasta Sauce Salad

Serves: *3*

Time: *15 minutes
(plus overnight soaking
and marinading time)*

Ingredients:

*100g salted sun-dried tomatoes
(plus water to soak)
1 apple
1 small courgette
½ small onion
1 level teaspoon ginger (grated)
½ lemon
6 teaspoons apple cider vinegar
3 tablespoons olive oil
25g olives (pitted)
1 small broccoli
1 small yellow sweet pepper
2 large courgettes (for 'noodles')*

This works well with raw courgette pasta or regular rice pasta noodles. I use a simple bit of equipment called a spiralizer to create noodles with courgette or carrot, but you can also create pasta strips using a potato peeler. Alternatively, this can be served as a sauce over a heap of delicious chopped salad leaves, grated carrot or regular pasta etc.

This recipe calls for 'dry' salted sun-dried tomatoes, rather than the type you find ready soaked in the jar. But just wing it if you can't get them.

After creating the pasta sauce, you chop the broccoli and salad ingredients, allowing them to marinade in the sauce for a few hours before serving. You can leave it for less time or serve straight away BUT allowing it to marinade really does help the flavours to dance and soften the broccoli, giving off the impression that it has been lightly cooked.

1. Soak tomatoes in water overnight (or for at least a few hours).
2. In the morning, drain the soak water from tomatoes, keeping 75ml of soak water and discarding the rest. Place soaked tomatoes and 75ml of the soak water into a big jug/ blender or food processor. If your sun-dried tomatoes are not pre-salted, then add a pinch of salt at this stage.
3. Chop apple and courgette into chunks (including skin, unless they are not organic).
4. Peel and chop onion.
5. Grate 1 level teaspoon's worth of ginger.
6. Juice half a lemon and discard the rind.
7. Add all ingredients (except the broccoli, pepper and courgettes) into the jug and blend until you achieve a sauce-like consistency. If it is too thick then add a little more water (taking care not to add too much).
8. Chop the broccoli and pepper into really small pieces and allow them to marinate in the sauce for a few hours before serving.
9. Turn your courgettes into noodles with a spiralizer or potato peeler.
10. Pour sauce over courgette noodles and enjoy.
11. Alternatively use over regular wheat-free pasta or veggies (raw or cooked).

I've learned that people will forget what you said,

people will forget what you did,

but people will never forget

how you made them feel.

Maya Angelou

Fennel Salad
with Cashew Cream

Serves: *2*

Time: *10 mins*
(plus soaking)

Ingredients:
1 lemon
50g (approx) cashews
2 teaspoons tamari
(or 1 teaspoon sea salt)
2 tablespoons water
1 fennel bulb
1 medium apple

Fennel is an aromatic herb. Used raw it has a mild licorice flavour and a crunchy bite, making it a perfect salad ingredient. It comes with some fantastic nutritional benefits and is naturally supportive to the digestive system, heart health, blood pressure, hormonal balance and bone health, so I like to make the most of it when it's in season. This is a tasty, creamy salad dish that works as an addition to a buffet or as a side on a big salad plate. The cashew cream is easy to make if you have a hand blender (the quantity is so small that you might struggle to blend it in a regular jug blender).

1. Juice the lemon, discarding pips and rind. Pour into a small jug along with the cashews, tamari and water. Leave to soak for a minimum of one hour to soften the cashews before blending (you can leave this for much longer, even overnight).
2. When ready to blend, use a hand blender to pulse whilst using a pushing down action to really get in there. Scrape off the blender as necessary.
3. Prepare the fennel as follows... if your fennel still has the stalks and fronds (feathery leaves) intact, then chop them off at the place where the bulb meets the stalks. Separate the feathery fronds from the stalks and put to the side (the stalks can be used in stews or soups later). Slice the bulb into quarters and remove the centre piece if it is really tough. Chop the rest of the bulb into small pieces.
4. Chop apple (with skin still on) into small pieces.
5. If you do have feathery fronds, save a handful to mix in and use as garnish (any more left over would add nicely to most salads over the next few days).
6. You are now ready to mix everything. Just toss all ingredients together until evenly coated. If the cream is too thick, add a splash more water to loosen up.
7. Garnish with a few fennel fronds and enjoy!

Summer Flower Kale Salad

Here's one of my favourite salad blends that I love to serve along with a delicious hemp oil salad dressing. Use my recipe for inspiration, but make the most of whatever you have available at the time. I love to grow edible flowers like nasturtiums or chives and adorn my summer salads with their colourful petals. This serves nicely with hummus too (see my Roasted Red Pepper Hummus recipe on page 64).

1. Make sure there aren't any tough stalks on your kale (tender stalks are fine - I always toss them into the salad) and roughly chop.
2. De-seed bell pepper and chop into small pieces.
3. Cut squares into the avocado flesh whilst still in the shell and then scoop into salad bowl along with all other ingredients, except the flowers.
4. Dress with my 'Hemp & Parsley Salad Dressing' (see page 56) and adorn with your edible summer flowers.

Serves: *1 - 2*

Time: *5 mins*

Ingredients:

Couple of handfuls of kale

½ a yellow sweet bell pepper

½ a ripe avocado

Small handful of cherry tomatoes

5 to 10 dried black olives

A few slices of cucumber

Handful of pea shoots

Few basil leaves (optional)

Edible summer flowers like nasturtiums or chive blossoms

Drizzle of Hemp & Parsley Dressing (see page 56)

Walnut & Sun-Dried Tomato Super Detox Salad

Serves: *2 - 4*

Time: *20 mins*
(plus soak time)

Sauce ingredients:

50g (a large handful) sun-dried tomatoes (with water to soak)

75g walnuts

2 tablespoons hemp oil

½ teaspoon ground turmeric

1 tablespoon raw apple cider vinegar

½ a medium-sized apple

10 tablespoons (approx) soak water from sun-dried tomatoes

Salad ingredients:

1 large carrot

½ to 1 small cauliflower

A few large kale leaves

A couple of handfuls of rocket

A sprinkle of fresh parsley

Apart from the appetizing taste, this particular salad is charged with a few nourishing gems.

Turmeric is a warming spice well-known for its potent antioxidant, anti-inflammatory, anti-cancer, detoxification qualities. Walnuts, also rich in antioxidants, come with a healthy dose of melatonin (helps regulate sleep), B-vitamins, vitamin E (of the gamma-tocopherol vitamin E variety, which is excellent for cardio-vascular health). I like to include sun-dried tomatoes, not only because they taste so good, but because they provide the welcome gift of lycopene, an antioxidant that has been repeatedly shown to protect our cells and DNA against free-radical damage. Once we toss in some cauliflower, carrot, kale, rocket (arugula), each brimming with a world of nutritional goodness of their own, we soon have an amazingly healthy, filling medley that tastes quite divine.

To create this salad we make a delicious thick sauce in which to immerse the main salad first.

1. Begin ahead of time by soaking the sun-dried tomatoes in fresh spring or filtered water for about three hours (or until soft enough to blend). You can often purchase pre-soaked sun-dried tomatoes, although I usually find that they come in oil or vinegar - they should work fine too if you take them out of the oil.
2. When your tomatoes are ready, drain and keep the soak water (you will need it again shortly).
3. Blend walnuts, hemp oil, soaked sun-dried tomatoes, turmeric, apple cider vinegar and apple in a jug together to create a thick pâté. I tend to use a hand (immersion) blender for this. It helps me press down the ingredients and scrape the blade easily until I achieve the right consistency. Add about 10 tablespoons of the soak water to make it into a thick sauce (this will make it easier to mix in with your salad). If you used pre-soaked tomatoes and don't have any soak water, then simply use fresh water instead.
4. Grate your carrot and chop the rest of your veggies, saving the parsley to sprinkle on top.
5. Mix the chopped salad in a bowl with the sauce, adding a little dash of water to loosen if you find the sauce too thick.
6. Enjoy on its own in a salad bowl or as a side dish with something like millet, quinoa, sweet potato wedges or rice.

Variations

- Instead of sauce, use it as a thick dip. So, don't add the extra 10 tablespoons of soak water to your sauce ingredients and instead serve as it comes, straight after blending, alongside a salad.
- If you don't like turmeric, or fancy a change, then try using fresh ginger instead.
- Be creative with whatever veggies you have available. This salad goes particularly well with any dense veggies. Try grated sweet potato, swede (rutabaga), celery, broccoli, sliced cabbage etc. as alternatives.

Serves: *2*

Time: *10 mins*

Salad ingredients:

1 large carrot
1 small apple
1 bell pepper
3 radishes (optional)
1 small bok choy
A few lettuce leaves
Sprinkle of macadamia nuts
Organic corn chips (optional)

Avocado sauce ingredients:

1 small lemon
2 cloves of garlic
1 medium ripe avocado
Small handful basil or coriander
Pinch of sea salt
2 teaspoons apple cider vinegar
1 teaspoon maple syrup

Hawaiian Avocado Garden Salad

One of my favourite things about going to Hawaii is the incredible taste of the avocados there. I prefer to eat them just as they come - right off the tree - as well as weaving them into salads. Avocados are one of my top five foods choices for optimal health and wellness with a myriad of different benefits.

1. For the sauce: juice the lemon, crush the garlic and then blend all sauce ingredients together in a blender. Alternatively mash avocado, juice lemon, crush garlic, roughly chop the coriander and then mash everything together with a fork.
2. Grate carrot.
3. Slice apple, bell pepper and radishes.
4. Chop the bok choy and lettuce leaves.
5. Toss everything together.
6. Garnish with a few nuts or radish slices.
7. Serve with organic corn chips (optional).

Roast Aubergine Salad

Aubergine has a desirable fleshy texture, a bit like oyster mushrooms. In this recipe I am using long, thin, Japanese aubergines. If you aren't able to get these, then just use whatever varieties you have available. This dish serves either warm or cold. Add in a few warming spices and we get to enjoy a unique and enjoyable salad recipe.

Roasting the aubergine:

1. Preheat oven to gas mark 7 (220°C/425°F).
2. Mix coconut oil, ginger, nutmeg, salt and vinegar together.
3. Dice aubergine into small centimetre cubes; toss into a mixing bowl and quickly (and thoroughly) mix with the coconut oil blend that you've just created.
4. Spread the coated aubergine on a large baking tray and bake for about 25 minutes.

Salad: whilst the aubergine is cooking, prepare the salad.

1. Peel and grate 1 teaspoon's worth of fresh ginger.
2. Grate beetroot and carrot.
3. Chop kale into small pieces.
4. Toss all salad ingredients with rice vinegar and flax oil.
5. When the aubergine is ready, toss into the salad when it is still warm (or allow to cool first if preferred).
6. Add the rocket leaves and sprinkle of hempseeds right at the end.

Serves: *2*

Time: *20 mins*

Aubergine Roast ingredients:

*2 long thin aubergines
(or equivalent)*
2 teaspoons coconut oil
Sprinkle ground ginger
Sprinkle freshly grated nutmeg
Big pinch celtic sea salt
2 teaspoons apple cider vinegar

Salad ingredients:

1 teaspoon ginger (freshly grated)
1 small beetroot
1 medium-sized carrot
1 large kale leaf
2 teaspoons rice vinegar
2 teaspoons flax oil
Sprinkle of hulled hempseeds
Handful of rocket

Spiced Curry Potato Salad

Potatoes come in all sorts of shapes, sizes and textures. When making a potato salad it is important to choose a variety of potato that holds together well with cooking. A low-starch, more waxy potato will do the trick. Use a good quality curry powder so that you can benefit from delicious healthful spices. This spicy potato salad keeps well for a few days in the fridge and really comes into its own as part of a colourful lunch time salad buffet.

Serves: 4

Time: *20 mins (plus cooling)*

Ingredients:

750g small new potatoes
Handful fresh parsley

Curry dressing:

1 clove garlic
1 teaspoon mild curry powder
1 tablespoon sunflower oil
Pinch of sea salt
1 teaspoon brown rice vinegar
1 teaspoon brown rice syrup

1. Chop the potatoes into small pieces between an inch and half an inch cubed - with skin still on.
2. Steam the potatoes until they are 'only just' cooked (but definitely not overcooked otherwise they will fall apart when you come to mix them with the curry dressing). When cooked, take them off the heat, and put them in a large, open, salad mixing bowl or large strainer. The reason for this is because they will continue to cook as long as they are still hot, even after you've strained them. So it's helpful to get them out of the hot pan.
3. Crush the clove of garlic and then mix all the dressing ingredients together.
4. Finely chop the parsley.
5. Mix the curry dressing with the potatoes until evenly coated throughout.
6. Gently mix in the parsley.
7. Allow to fully cool and then refrigerate until ready to serve.

Super Healthy Raw-Slaw

This is a crunchy, appetizing alternative to traditional 'coleslaw'. It serves well as part of a salad buffet, as a cracker topping, a sandwich filling or a side dish... It benefits from the incredible health-affirming goodness of fennel and celery, along with a tasteful combination of wholesome ingredients to create a creamy tahini sauce.

1. Slice the celery into small slices (using leaves too, if there are any).
2. Grate carrot.
3. Chop and thinly slice the fennel (removing any tough outer layers).
4. Make the sauce by chopping the apple, juicing the lemon, then blending together with a hand blender in a small jug with all other sauce ingredients to make a thick creamy sauce.
5. Mix sauce in with the vegetables thoroughly. If the sauce thickens up too much, simply add a little more water and mix in.
6. Sprinkle with your favourite seeds and serve.

Serves: *2*

Time: *10 mins*

Salad ingredients:
4 large celery stalks
1 large carrot
1 small (200g) fennel
1 small ripe avocado or a handful of olives (optional)

Sauce Ingredients:
1 small apple
1 lemon (juiced)
1 heaped teaspoon mustard (the jarred type of mustard)
3 tablespoons tahini
4 tablespoons water
1 teaspoon sea salt
1 teaspoon caraway seeds (optional)
Small handful of seeds

Pâtés, Dips & Dressings

Hemp & Parsley Salad Dressing

Time: *5 mins*

Ingredients:

150ml cold-pressed hemp oil
75ml apple cider vinegar
1 large clove of garlic
1 heaped teaspoon of organic mustard (ready made type in a jar)
1 handful of fresh parsley
1 tablespoon of tamari (or ½ teaspoon sea salt)
Dash of maple syrup/rice syrup

When I go to the effort of making a salad dressing, I like to make a large batch, so that I can enjoy it on my salads all week long. I love to use cold-pressed hemp oil in my dressings because it is super nutritious and has an impressive blend of essential fats. If you do buy hemp oil, it's important to find a good quality one - both for taste and nutritional benefits (the same goes for all oils actually). I use other oils for this recipe too - this dressing would work well with flax, sunflower or olive oils as an alternative.

The best way to make this is to blend all these ingredients together for a few seconds in a jug with a hand blender or to use a regular blender. Alternatively, you can crush the garlic, finely chop the parsley and give it a really good whisk with a fork. I prefer to blend this one, to get everything to infuse together quickly. Blending gives it a bit of rapid pazzazz whilst helping it all hold together as one delicious dressing.

ABOUT HEMPSEED OIL & HEMPSEEDS

Hempseed oil is the main oil I use for salad dressings. The best hempseed oil will have a green tint along with a fresh, nutty flavour. Choose a cold-pressed, unrefined oil to ensure that it retains its optimal goodness. It is known to be unstable at high temperatures, therefore, it is not advisable to use for frying or baking. It works well by drizzling over potatoes or veggies after cooking and is always my first choice for salad dressings.

You will also notice that I use hulled/shelled hempseeds (also known as hempseed hearts) from time to time too (the seeds in the picture to the right still have their hulls on). They have a light, nutty flavour and blend easily into smoothies or act as a great sprinkle for salad and cereals. Grind them or use them whole. Hempseeds and their oil are one of the most amazing seeds gifted to humanity. Culinary grade hemp is different to marijuana and contains a completely insignificant amount of THC (delta 9 tetrahydrocannabinol - the primary psychoactive ingredient in marijuana that gets people 'high').

Hemp is one of the most complete proteins in the plant food kingdom, containing ALL 21 known amino acids. It contains nature's perfect ratio (3:1) of omega-3 to omega-6 essentially fatty acids, and is an excellent source of GLA (gamma linolenic acid). Hemp has been shown to help people with skin disorders, PMS, menopause, cancer, heart disease, arthritis and has good anti-inflammatory benefits. Hempseeds are high in the antioxidant vitamin E. This powerful plant has also been found to contain tocopherol, which has benefits for those with both Alzheimer's and atherosclerosis. Phytol is another helpful hempseed antioxidant, which is known to have anti-cancer properties.

Lemon Balm, Pumpkin Seed Pâté

Lemon Balm, also known as *Melissa officinalis*, springs up all over my garden in abundance early in the year, with very little attention. It scatters out the most bountiful harvest at a time when other greens are just starting to unfurl their leaves. It thrives in most places, taking care of itself rather well, spreading vigorously with its roots and seeds, offering some rather remarkable health benefits along the way (most notably used for its calming effect on the nervous and digestive systems).

I regularly grab handfuls of the stuff, slicing and chopping it for salads, desserts and invigorating herbal tea infusions. Another way I love to bring it into our diet is through this delicious pâté. It's so tasty on an oatcake or used as a dip for carrot and celery sticks. We enjoy it at lunch time along with a nice fresh, hearty salad.

You will need a blender for this. I prefer a hand blender, so that I can get right in there as I press down.

Time: *5 mins*
(plus 3 hours soaking)

Ingredients:
100g Pumpkin Seeds
1 heaped teaspoon of ginger
½ apple (medium)
1 lemon (juiced)
1 handful fresh lemon balm
2 tablespoons olive oil
½ teaspoon sea salt

1. Soak pumpkin seeds in spring or filtered water for at least 3 hours to soften.
2. After soaking, drain, discard soak water and place pumpkin seeds in a jug for blending.
3. Peel and finely chop 1 heaped teaspoon's worth of fresh ginger.
4. Roughly chop your apple and juice lemon.
5. Add all ingredients together and blend in the jug until you achieve desired consistency. You'll probably end up with a great, rustic looking pâté, rather than an ultra smooth dip.
6. Serve straight away. It should also keep in the fridge for a few days.

Simple Tahini Dressing

This is a simple, oil-free tahini dressing that works well with any sort of salad. Add extra chopped herbs if you want to vary it a little.

Time: *3 mins*

Ingredients:
1 small lemon
4 tablespoons tahini
1 small garlic clove
Salt to taste
Water to thin

1. Juice the lemon and slowly mix in with the tahini. It sometimes takes a while for the tahini to achieve a creamy consistency, but if you keep at it, it will work a dream.
2. Crush the garlic and add along with a big pinch of salt.
3. If you want it thinner, just add a little water at a time until you achieve your desired consistency.

About Tahini

Tahini is a paste/butter made from sesame seeds. Taste and texture varies a lot from brand to brand, so be sure to find one that you really like. Ideally your tahini won't taste too bitter and will have a pleasing creamy texture that is easy to dip a spoon into. If your jar has been stored for a long time you may find that the oil rises and the thicker bulk of the tahini settles to the bottom. If this happens, take a little time to stir it in with a knife or spoon before you start using it. This may take a little while, but it is well worth it for ideal consistency and creaminess.

Perfect Guacamole

Time: *5 mins*

Ingredients:

1 large ripe avocado
1 small lime or lemon
¼ teaspoon sea salt
Pinch ground coriander
Several cherry tomatoes
¼ small red onion
Small handful of coriander leaves

Guacamole is thought to have originated in Aztec Mexico, evolving from whatever was available locally. Most people I know adore the rich, fatty, creaminess of avocado and are delighted to see it show up at meal times. Avocados are laden with health benefits, so it is no wonder that they rank at the top of every discerning health seeker's menu.

Guacamole comes in many different variations. The limit is your imagination as long as you use good quality ingredients and a ripe avocado. Here is one of my favourite guacamole creations…

1. Dice or scoop out your avocado.
2. Juice lemon or lime and add to the avocado in a bowl.
3. Add salt and ground coriander then mash avocado with a fork.
4. Quarter your cherry tomatoes and finely chop onion with a sharp knife.
5. Roughly chop (or tear) coriander (cilantro) leaves (I include the stalks too - seems a waste not to).
6. Mix all remaining ingredients into the bowl with a fork until you reach your desired consistency. Some people do prefer to blend to a smooth spread with a blender. I prefer a rustic, mashed, chunky dip.
7. Enjoy with salad, in a wrap, in a sandwich, with baked potatoes, on crackers or rice cakes. It's pretty versatile.

Alternative
Substitute coriander leaves with basil - delicious!

Walnut & Coriander Pâté

When every bite of your lunch is filled with nutrient-rich goodness you know you are doing yourself a real service. Walnuts are thought to be the healthiest nut available, with superior antioxidant levels and a particularly high offering of vitamin E. 25g of walnuts can provide a whopping 90% of the recommended daily intake of omega-3 essential fat. Then there's coriander - a herbal superstar, with excellent antimicrobial, antioxidant, anti-fungal, anti-inflammatory properties as well as great levels of vitamins K, C & A, iron, calcium, potassium and manganese (to name a few). Coriander is said to be good at removing heavy metals such as mercury, cadmium, lead and aluminium from the body, which is more than enough to earn itself a regular invitation to my lunch table. In today's world of pollution and toxins we can really use all the help we can get to maintain optimum health. I enjoy this pâté along with a tasty salad at lunch time...

Serves: *2*

Time: *5 mins*
(plus 3 hours soaking)

Ingredients:
50g walnuts
½ lemon (juiced)
½ small apple
Small handful coriander leaves
Pinch sea salt

1. Soak walnuts in water overnight (or for at least 3 hours) to soften for blending.
2. After soaking, rinse walnuts until the water runs clear.
3. Juice lemon and compost the left over skin.
4. Chop apple into small chunks (including skin).
5. Use a blender to blend all ingredients together (scraping/ clearing the blade as necessary) until a pâté has formed.

Bring-da Ginger Pâté

Time: *5 mins*

(plus 3 hours soak time)

Ingredients:

100g Sunflower seeds

25g pumpkin seeds

Small handful sun-dried tomatoes

½ inch cubed of fresh ginger

Small handful of coriander leaves

2 tablespoons apple cider vinegar

1½ tablespoons olive or hemp oil

Squeeze of lemon

Pinch of sea salt (only if sun-dried tomatoes are NOT salted)

I love soaking seeds overnight to soften them and then blend to make a rich, healthy pâté. Soaking seeds before you use them unleashes their incredible life force, which not only makes them easier to digest, but infuses you with high vibrational energy. The ginger and sun-dried tomatoes give this pâté a delightful tanginess, whilst the seeds cream together to create a gorgeous blend of essential fats - necessary for good health.

1. You will need to soak sunflower and pumpkin seeds in water overnight, or for at least 3 hours, to soften them. Unless your sun-dried tomatoes have already been soaked, pop them in to the soak water along with the seeds. Make sure there is more than twice the volume of water compared to the seeds and tomatoes.
2. When ready, drain the seeds and sun-dried tomatoes.
3. Peel and finely grate the ginger.
4. Put ginger into a jug along with the drained seeds, sun-dried tomatoes and all remaining ingredients. Use a hand blender, so that you can push downward and apply pressure. If you use a regular blender, then pulsate and keep stopping to scrape down the sides. Add salt if needed. It's ready when you have a pâté-type consistency.

Parsley Pesto

This is a lovely alternative to pesto that serves nicely with salad. It also goes well with rice cakes, oatcakes or as part of a salad sandwich. As a variation you could use either all sunflower or all pumpkin seeds (rather than 50/50).

1. Ahead of time: soak sunflower and pumpkin seeds for at least 3 hours in fresh water. This softens them for blending as well as making them much easier to digest. It works well to soak them even longer than 3 hours if you have the time. I often soak them overnight.
2. When ready to make the pesto, crush the garlic and juice the lemon.
3. Add all ingredients to a jug and blend until you achieve desired pesto-like consistency.
4. Enjoy.

Time: *5 mins*
(plus 3 hours soak time)

Ingredients:
50g sunflower seeds
50g pumpkin seeds
1 large clove garlic
1 lemon (juiced)
Handful fresh parsley
¼ teaspoon sea salt
2 tablespoons olive oil
1 teaspoon tamari

ROAST RED PEPPER HUMMUS

Serves: *4 big portions*

Time: *30 mins*

Ingredients:

2 large sweet red bell peppers
2 large cloves of garlic
200g chickpeas
2 lemons
2 heaped tablespoons of tahini
3 tablespoons virgin olive oil
½ teaspoon sea salt

Hummus is a delicious plant-based dip that first emerged from the Middle East. With growing awareness of health and wellness it has rapidly gained popularity in other parts of the world too (especially in my house!). In addition to regular hummus ingredients, my variation of the traditional version brings in the tantalising sweetness of roasted sweet pepper. It gives an awesome combination of beneficial nutrients too…

- Sesame seeds (puréed - in the form of tahini) are rich in healthy fats and minerals.
- Chickpeas (garbanzo beans) are high in protein as well as having plentiful manganese, copper, phosphorus, iron and folic acid.
- Sweet pepper has mega levels of vitamin C.
- Lemon and garlic both offer powerful antioxidant, anti-bacterial and immune boosting properties.

I was interested in creating a really appetising version of hummus - one where the flavours alchemically transform to provide a wonderful infusion of deliciousness. So, I decided to roast the sweet pepper and garlic, since roasting certainly unleashes the incredible fullness of these flavoursome foods.

1. De-seed, de-stalk and slice your peppers in half or quarters.
Next, roast the sweet pepper and garlic in a hot oven... To do this, keep the garlic in its skin and place on an oven tray along with the pepper. Place the tray in a preheated oven at about gas mark 7 (220°C/425°F). Roast the garlic for 10 minutes and the pepper for about 15-20 minutes (or until the pepper is easy to pierce). There's no need to let the pepper char. **Note:** I find it easier to roast this ahead of time - get on with something else - and then set them out to cool for a little while before adding to the rest of the ingredients.
2. It is best to wait until the garlic cools down a little before you pop it out of its skin. Gently chop off the top, then squeeze out the fleshy garlic and place in a jug ready to blend with everything else.
3. Rinse and drain the chickpeas.
4. Juice the lemons and discard the skin.
5. Add all ingredients to a jug and blend until you reach your desired consistency.
6. Chill in the fridge before serving.

Serving Suggestions:

- This serves well with salad, in a sandwich, on crackers, as a veggie dip, with baked potatoes or sweet potatoes wedges.
- It's pretty versatile and should keep in the fridge for over a week.
- I like to make a batch of pâtés and dips to enjoy throughout the week. Gotta make plenty in my house though as it seems to vanish pretty quickly!

Zingy Mint Inspired Salad Dressing

Time: *5 mins*

Ingredients:

Handful of fresh garden mint
½ medium-sized apple
3 tablespoons of rice vinegar
2 tablespoons flax oil
3 tablespoons olive oil
1 teaspoon maple syrup (optional)

Mint lends itself well to salad dishes and dressings. It has a uniquely refreshing, playful taste that can liven up a plate of leaves and other veggies in no time. Mint is super healthy. So, quite apart from its lovely taste and fanfare of nutrients, it is one of my favourite herbs for adding to all sorts of dishes. It's good for soothing digestion issues; helping against nausea and headaches; supportive for respiratory disorders, coughs and asthma; and is even said to act as a natural stimulant against fatigue and depression.

1. De-stalk the mint.
2. Chop the apple into small chunks (peeled or unpeeled).
3. Blend all of the ingredients together in a blender.
4. Use as a salad dressing as desired.
5. This should keep for several days in the fridge.

Coriander Inspired Tahini Sauce

This sauce works nicely with falafel, chickpea burgers or as dressing for a potato or bean salad. The tahini gives it a gorgeous thick creaminess whilst the coriander leaves (also known as cilantro) infuses it with a mild, flavoursome warmth. Coriander is a popular culinary herb all over the world and this recipe benefits from both its ground seed and leaves.

1. Crush the garlic clove and then put in a jug and blend with all the other ingredients. Personally, I do this in a small beaker, using my hand blender. It should blend into a perfect sauce within a few seconds.
2. The amount of water you need will vary, depending on the consistency of tahini that you use.

Time: *5 mins*

Ingredients:
1 small garlic clove
4 tablespoons tahini
3 to 4 tablespoons water
2 teaspoons apple cider vinegar
¼ teaspoon celtic sea salt
½ teaspoon ground coriander
Small handful coriander leaves

Cashew Cream 'Cheeze' - 4 Ways

Cashew and lemon dance together in a way that makes a base for a good cream cheese alternative. There are lots of different variations for this, so once you have the basics (cashew nuts, lemon and salt) then the world of cashew cream 'cheeze' is yours to be discovered. It works as a spread on crackers, in a sandwich or as a stuffing for oven baked potatoes. For simplicity and speed I prefer to use a hand blender to blend this recipe - rather than a jug blender. If you want to use a jug blender then be prepared to keep scraping down the sides to keep it mixing. Here are some of my favourite easy cashew cheeze recipes. They keep well in the fridge for a few days...

Classic cashew cream cheeze

100g cashew nuts
1 very large lemon (juiced 75 - 100ml)
½ teaspoon celtic sea salt
Pinch of black pepper (optional)
Extra water for desired creamy consistency

1. Juice the lemon and leave with ingredients in a jug to soak overnight (or for a few hours). The lemon juice will soften the cashews for blending.
2. Once soaked, blend ingredients together until creamy smooth. If you need a little extra water to make it thinner or creamier then add a little at a time and blend.

Cashew olive cream cheeze

100g cashew nuts
1½ tablespoons apple cider vinegar
2 tablespoons water
1 large garlic clove
7 pitted dried black olives

1. Soak the cashew nuts in the apple cider vinegar and water overnight.
2. Crush the garlic.
3. Add the pitted olives and garlic when ready
   and then blend until creamy smooth.

Tomato sun-burst cheeze

100g cashew nuts
3 dry (salted) sun-dried tomatoes
1 small garlic clove
Water to soak
1 small lemon (juiced)
½ teaspoon celtic sea salt (only if sun-dried
tomatoes are NOT salted)

1. Crush garlic and soak with the cashews and sun-dried tomatoes in water (or for at least 3 hours).
2. Drain away the soak water.
3. If your sun-dried tomatoes are not pre-salted then add salt.
4. Juice the lemon.
5. Blend ingredients together to create a creamy smooth spread.

Cheeze n' chive cashew cream

100g cashew nuts
1 large lemon (juiced)
1 handful of chopped chives
1 small garlic clove (optional)
½ teaspoon celtic sea salt
Extra water for desired creamy consistency
1 teaspoon finely chopped chives (extra)

1. Soak cashews in the lemon juice overnight (or for at least 3 hours).
2. When ready, add all ingredients to blending jug (keeping back the teaspoon of chives to mix in once blended).
3. Blend until creamy smooth, adding a little extra water if needed.
4. Mix in the teaspoon of chives at the end and serve.

Soups

Sweet Roast Pepper Soup

Sweet bell pepper comes completely into its own when roasted. It brings out a sweet, aromatic depth lending itself beautifully to this roasted red pepper soup. Full of healthful antioxidants like vitamin C. It is delicious.

Serves: *2*

Time: *40 mins*

Ingredients:
4 red peppers
4 large plum tomatoes
3 cloves garlic
1 medium sweet potato
1 courgette
75g red lentils
500ml water
1 teaspoon sea salt
Large handful of parsley
150ml coconut cream (optional)

1. Preheat the oven to gas mark 6 (200°C/400°F).
2. De-seed and slice the red peppers into quarters and place on a baking tray with the whole plum tomatoes.
3. Separate the garlic cloves from the bulb, removing any 'loose' skin, but being sure to leave on a layer of skin. Slice off the tip of the root end of the garlic and place on the baking tray with the peppers and tomatoes.
4. Bake for about 20 minutes.
5. In the meantime, whilst waiting for the peppers, tomatoes and garlic to roast, dice the sweet potato and courgette into small cubes and place into a medium-sized pan with the lentils, water and sea salt.
6. When the peppers, tomatoes and garlic are ready, take them out of the oven and place the peppers and tomatoes into the soup pan along with the other ingredients (except garlic). Bring pan to the boil. Once bubbling, reduce to a simmer and cook for up to 20 minutes.
7. It's best to let the garlic cool for a few minutes before adding to the pan (it's very hot underneath that skin!). Once it's cool enough to handle, squeeze out the garlic flesh, discard the skin and add to the rest of the ingredients in the pan.
8. Once the soup is cooked, chop parsley and toss into the pan. Use a hand blender to pulse through the soup a few times to achieve your desired, rustic consistency.
9. Stir in coconut cream if desired, for extra creaminess.

Roast Cashew Soup

Most of the time involved in creating this soup is spent waiting for things to bake and cook quietly in the background, whilst you can be getting on with something else in the kitchen. The roast cashew in this is a real gift as it entwines it's rich, silken earthiness amidst the other ingredients. With ginger, coriander, roast garlic and squash, it creates an exciting feast of gently sweet, aromatic and delectable deliciousness.

1. Halve the butternut squash and scoop out the seeds. Bake in a preheated oven at gas mark 7 (220°C/425°F) for about an hour.
2. Evenly spread the cashews on a baking tray and bake in the oven for about 15 minutes (or until tanned).
3. Bake the garlic in the oven for 15 minutes (keeping on the skin for now).

In the meantime...
1. Slice the celery stalk and pop into a pan.
2. Finely grate a heaped teaspoon's worth of ginger and add to the pan along with the ground coriander, sea salt and water. Put to the side until the other ingredients have baked.
3. When ready pop the garlic out of its skin. Add to the pan.
4. Scoop the butternut squash out of its skin. Add to the pan.
5. Toss in the cashews, turn on the heat and let the pan cook for up to 25 minutes.
6. When cooking time is over, blend contents until smooth and serve.

Serves: *2 - 3*

Time: *90 mins*

Ingredients:
1 butternut squash (750g to 1kg)
75g cashews
3 large garlic cloves
1 large celery stalk
1 heaped teaspoon ginger (grated)
1 heaped tablespoon ground coriander
1 teaspoon celtic sea salt
600ml water
Few sprigs of parsley (optional)

TASTE OF EDEN SOUP

This is delicious and fragrant - the sort of soup that comes naturally to me when I feel like having a nice, well-rounded, quick meal in one pot. This blend has a fine medley of vitamins, minerals, protein and health-promoting goodness to keep you well-nourished and satisfied. It's very tasty and quick. Be sure to use a good quality, full-fat, organic coconut milk for optimal results.

Serves: 3

Time: *30 mins*

Ingredients:
2 large sweet potatoes
1 heaped teaspoon fresh ginger
5 green cardamom pods
100g cooked chickpeas
100g mushrooms
400ml tin full-fat coconut milk
Big pinch celtic sea salt
100ml water
2 handfuls of spinach
Handful of basil

1. Chop sweet potato into small chunks somewhere between 1cm and 2cm cubed in size.
2. Peel and grate a heaped teaspoon's worth of ginger.
3. Open the cardamom pods (discard the shells) and crush the seeds. This is easy to do with a sharp, heavy knife by chopping repeatedly over and over the seeds, or even better, use a pestle and mortar.
4. Drain and rinse the chickpeas (if you are using them straight from a can).
5. Chop the mushrooms.
6. Toss all ingredients in the pan together (except the basil and spinach) and bring to the boil before reducing to a simmer. Allow to cook for approximately 25 minutes or until the sweet potatoes are easy to pierce with a fork and just beginning to fall apart.
7. Toss the spinach leaves in right at the end of the cooking period. If the spinach is in large leaves then roughly chop before tossing into the pan. Mix into the soup, whilst encouraging the sweet potatoes to slightly fall apart. This will help to thicken the coconut milk and turn it into more of a cream.
8. Chop the basil leaves. To preserve the basil flavour, it is best to add the basil leaves just before you serve, once the soup is off the heat. Simply mix in and then serve.

Celeriac & Coconut Soup
(with kaffir lime leaves and lemongrass)

If you mention celeriac to most people, you'll likely see a confused 'haven't-got-a-clue' look. Like its cousin celery, celeriac is a member the parsnip family (it does however look more like a curious, wild and knobbly version of turnip than celery). At first glance it can be a little bit off-putting, although if your adventuresome spirit dares you to try it once, you may be a friend of celeriac forever. It's low in starch (unlike most other root veggies) and makes a good alternative to mashed potatoes. The flesh inside is white, whilst the flavour is somewhat gentle and celery-like. Celeriac is commonly cultivated in Northern Europe and the Mediterranean, but you can find it in organic farmers' markets and healthy grocery shops all over the world these days.

In this soup I use dried kaffir lime leaves and lemon grass (available in good health food and herb shops) to bring a gentle infusion of Asian flavours into the blend. You will need a 'tea leaf ball infuser' (or similar) for the kaffir lime leaves in this recipe and a blender.

1. Dried lemongrass benefits from being softened before cooking. If you have time, soak it (overnight, a few hours or as long as you have) in a little amount of water.
2. Scrub and peel the celeriac. You will need to chop off all the knobbly root parts and skin with a sharp knife. Chop up the remaining white root and place into a medium-sized cooking pot.
3. Roughly chop your celery stalks, including all leaves and add to the pot along with the water, coconut milk, salt and lemongrass.
4. Bring pot to the boil.
5. Cram your kaffir lime leaves into the tea infuser ball and drop it into your pot. The reason that it's a good idea to do this with an infuser ball is because you will need to take out the lime leaves before blending. You can drop the leaves in without a ball, but you'll need to remember to find them and scoop out before blending. They are used for flavour, rather than eating.
6. Once your soup has come to the boil, turn down the heat and allow to simmer gently for about 25 minutes.

Serves: 3

Time: 40 mins

Ingredients:

1 heaped teaspoon dried lemongrass

500g celeriac (peeled weight approx)

6 to 8 large celery stalks

400ml water

400ml coconut milk

1 teaspoon sea salt

5 dried kaffir lime leaves

Celtic Leek & Potato Soup
(infused with Rosemary & Thyme)

Serves: *8*

Time: *25 mins*

Ingredients:

2 large leeks
Splash of olive oil
1.25 litres water
1 heaped teaspoon sea salt
2 generous rosemary stalks
1 heaped tablespoon fresh thyme
1.25kg potatoes
1 large sweet potato (350g)
Parsley (optional)

When winter starts settling in, I always welcome something warm and hearty to my menu. I felt inspired to create this thick soul-warming soup one chilly day, as I watched the Avalonian mists dance outside my kitchen window in Glastonbury. Leek and potato soup is a traditional soup in Celtic lands, warming you right through to the core. In this version I also add fresh rosemary, garden thyme and sweet potato for a divine infusion of flavours.

1. Chop leeks and sauté in a large cooking pot with the oil for two or three minutes, stirring a few times during the process. After two or three minutes pour in all of the water and salt and bring to the boil.
2. In the meantime, de-stalk and finely chop your rosemary (as fine as you can anyway). De-stalk the thyme and toss it into the pan along with the rosemary. You should have about 2 heaped tablespoons of rosemary when finely chopped.
3. Chop potatoes (skins still on - best part!) and sweet potato (skin still on) into small pieces and add to the pan. By this time, the water should be starting to boil. Turn down to a simmer and allow to cook for at least 20 minutes (or until the potatoes are cooked).
4. You might like to let the potatoes start to fall apart a little. This adds a wonderful thickness to the soup.
5. Add some chopped parsley at the end or garnish each bowl with a sprinkle (if you have some - optional).

Sweet Potato & Lentil Stew

This is a hearty stew, although it can be served as a soup too. It's a simple one-pot meal with an exciting and satisfying medley of flavours.

1. Crush or finely chop garlic. Roughly chop onion and sauté them both in a big pan with a dash of olive oil for 2 or 3 minutes.
2. Chop sweet potato into small chunks (1½cm cubed or slightly larger is ideal) - leaving skins on. Toss into the pan along with the sautéed onion and garlic. Add water, passata, red lentils, salt and bring back to the boil.
3. In the meantime, crack open cardamom pods on a chopping board, removing the husks. Go over with a sharp knife quickly to chop/crush and unleash their flavour (or try grinding with a pestle & mortar if you prefer). Toss into the cooking pot.
4. Once boiling, turn the pot down to a simmer and stir occasionally throughout the cooking period. Cook for about 30 minutes.
5. Roughly chop creamed coconut block. Toss into the pot at any time and stir in as it melts.
6. Chop the kale into small pieces and add about 10 minutes before the completion of cooking time.
7. Serve by itself for a filling stew or enjoy with some of your favourite chunky bread or oatcakes.

Serves: *4*

Time: *35 mins*

Ingredients:

2 large cloves garlic
1 large onion
Dash olive oil
700g sweet potato
700ml water
500ml passata
150g red lentils
1 teaspoon sea salt
5 cardamom pods
150g creamed coconut block
150g kale

Mushroom & Cardamom Squash Soup

Serves: *2 hearty bowls*

Time: *30 mins*

Ingredients:

350g of peeled squash
4 cardamom pods
1 heaped teaspoon ginger (grated)
300 - 400ml water
125ml coconut cream
250ml passata
1 teaspoon celtic sea salt
1 medium-sized leek
200g mushrooms
Dash of coconut oil
A handful of fresh herbs (either parsley or basil)

This is a perfect autumn squash recipe for chilly evenings, snuggled around an open fire. The inviting fragrance of cardamom, warming hint of ginger, earthy mushrooms, tomato, coconut and fresh herbs weave together to create a delightfully pleasing soup. I use the seeds from the cardamom pods, which imbue a richer, more aromatic flavour than its pre-ground version. Cardamom and ginger (like many quality herbs and spices) unleash a myriad of health benefits. As Hippocrates once said: 'let food be thy medicine'.

Any sort of mushrooms will work here, although I prefer flavourful ones like chestnut or even shiitake. You will need two pans for this recipe. It is simple to make, created in two parts that are combined together, making one delicious soup. The first part involves creating a squash sauce/soup base. While that is cooking, you will need to sauté the leek and mushrooms separately.

1. Peel and dice approximately 350g of squash. Chopping into cubes (under an inch cubed in size will work fine).
2. Open your cardamom pods and take out the seeds. Finely chop these seeds with a sharp knife by going over and over them and scraping your tiny pile back to centre a few times, until the seeds seem well chopped.
3. Peel and finely grate 1 heaped teaspoon's worth of fresh ginger.
4. Add the cardamom and ginger to your squash pan with the water, coconut cream, passata and sea salt. Bring to the boil, then allow to simmer for at least 15 minutes (or until the squash is soft enough to easily pierce with a fork).
5. Blend until smooth, with a hand blender if you have one, or blend in a jug blender.

Cooking the leek and mushroom:
1. Whilst you are waiting for the squash to cook... melt a dash of coconut oil in a pan and turn on the heat.
2. Roughly chop your mushrooms and chop leeks quite small.
3. Add to the pan and gently sauté for a few minutes until soft.

Bringing it all together:
Add the mushroom and leek into the main squash base and gently mix in along with a generous handful of freshly chopped basil or parsley.

Shiitake Beetroot Soup

Serves: 3

Time: *20 mins*

Ingredients:

*2 small/medium beetroots
(about 300g)*
800ml water
400g squash or pumpkin
1 to 2cm cubed of ginger
1 medium-sized leek
100g shiitake mushrooms
½ teaspoon sea salt
100g creamed coconut block *
*Small handful cashews
(optional extra)*

This super healthy soup is a great way to make the most of seasonal beetroot whilst embracing its amazing colour. I like to use shiitake mushrooms with this blend, for their smoky flavour and fantastic immune support, although you can easily replace with whatever mushrooms you have available. The creamed coconut (which comes in solid block form) is also a key element to this soup, bringing a rich infusion of coconut flavour and extra creaminess.

1. Scrub the beetroot (leaving skin on) and chop into small chunks, before tossing into a medium-sized pan. Add the water, place the lid on the pan and turn on the heat.
2. Peel the squash, chop into small pieces and toss into the pan.
3. Finely chop the ginger and roughly chop leek, before adding to the pan along with the shiitake mushrooms and salt.
4. Once it has come to the boil, turn down to gently simmer for about 20 minutes.
5. Near the end of the cooking time roughly chop the creamed coconut block and add to the pan. Stir in to encourage it to melt.
6. Once cooked (when you can easily pierce a fork through the beetroot) turn off the heat and blend soup. I find a hand blender useful for this (so that I can keep the soup in the pan) although a jug blender will work well too.
7. Once served, sprinkle a few cashews on top of each bowl of soup (as an optional extra) and enjoy with your favourite bread.

* If you can't find creamed coconut block, try using coconut cream instead. Try 250ml of coconut cream as a replacement and ONLY 600ml of water.

CAULIFLOWER & CHICKPEA SOUP

Cauliflower is packed with wholesome, high vibrational goodness, so I include it in my weekly cuisine in ample amounts whenever it's in season. I love it raw, cooked in soups and curries, or gently steamed and served on a soft bed of quinoa with hemp oil & tamari (nothing beats a bit of good old fashioned simplicity). In this recipe I've used cauliflower to make a hearty soup. The coconut and tomato dance and twirl through the cauliflower and chickpeas to provide a lip-lickin' nurturing meal. It's simple (less is definitely more in this case) and incredibly satisfying.

1. Chop the onion and sauté in a medium-sized pan with oil for a couple of minutes.
2. Chop the cauliflower and any tender cauliflower leaves, then toss into the pan, adding all other remaining ingredients.
3. Bring to the boil and gently cook for about 20 minutes (or until the cauliflower is soft).
4. Take off the heat. If you have a hand blender then pop it in the pan and pulsate the blade with one or two quick presses. Or use a regular jug blender by scooping a couple of ladles' worth in and giving it a whirl before adding it back to the remaining soup. Blending like this gives the soup a more desirable thickness. However, should you find the blending thing too faffy, then just serve it as it is. Blending is not compulsory.
5. Finally, gently tear the basil, toss in the pan, give a quick stir and then serve.

Serves: 4

Time: *30 mins*

Ingredients:

1 medium onion
Drizzle of olive or coconut oil
1 small cauliflower with leaves
300ml spring water
250ml passata
125ml coconut cream
100g chickpeas (about ½ a tin)
1 teaspoon celtic sea salt
Small handful of fresh basil

Alternatives

Coconut: if you don't have coconut cream, use 50g of coconut block instead, or use organic coconut milk from a can (but if you do use milk, be sure to leave out most of the spring water from the recipe because milk is generally rather liquidy). Different forms of coconut yield different results, so be sure to play and explore.

Chickpeas: use butter beans or even sweet potatoes for a tasty variation.

Herbs: you might prefer coriander leaves or parsley instead of basil. The soup is versatile.

Passata: passata is tomato that has been cooked and sieved (often found bottled or in a carton). I love using it in soups. Your own baked tomatoes would work fine as an alternative to passata. If I have a nice crop of fresh tomatoes in the summer, I bake them, blend them and make my own version.

WHICH CULINARY COCONUT TO USE?

I am a massive fan of coconut in all of its myriad of different forms. It lends itself perfectly to healthy cuisine adding a thick, plant-based creaminess to soups, desserts, breakfasts and sauces. It has an exotic flavour that everyone is familiar with and most people love. It is essential to buy a good quality coconut product. Here are the main types available...

CREAMED COCONUT (not to be confused with 'coconut cream') comes in a pure, solid, concentrated block that melts on heating. It is the unsweetened, dehydrated fresh meat of a mature coconut that has been ground in to a semi-solid white cream. It solidifies at normal room temperature. Chop it up or grate before adding to your dishes. You can find it along with coconut milk in health food stores and it is often available in the world food section of a supermarket too. It adds an intense infusion of coconut flavour to soups and curries and can often help to thicken sauces. Creamed coconut is also the essential ingredient for my chocolate coconut fudge. Creamed coconut is very similar to coconut butter (which is different again to coconut oil) - it is, however, less expensive to buy than the butter version.

FRESH COCONUT yields a deliciously refreshing translucent water. When you crack open a young coconut, you'll find a very soft, almost translucent, jelly-like flesh. As coconuts mature, the flesh turns white in colour (rather than transparent) and becomes firm, yet still soft enough to slice a spoon through. The water doesn't usually taste that great in old coconuts and the flesh eventually turns hard, being inedible without processing.

COCONUT CREAM comes in a small can or carton and, if it is a good quality version, the cream will often separate from the coconut water. So be sure to mix it in before use. Coconut cream is like a thick pouring cream that works well in soups and other dishes.

COCONUT MILK usually comes in a can in the western world. It is made by grating the white flesh and soaking it in hot water. The cream rises to the top and is skimmed off (that's how you get coconut cream). The rest of the liquid is squeezed through a muslin cloth to extract the white liquid, known as coconut milk. A good quality coconut milk will be made with at least 55% coconut and the rest will be water (most brands do add a thickening agent, although if you can, find and use one without). Good quality coconut milks usually separate creating a thick cream on the top half. Just give them a stir or shake before using. Alternatively, just use the cream (ideal if you can't find coconut cream).

COCONUT SUGAR/NECTAR is taken from the sap of the coconut flower. It's a healthy sweetener, and, unlike refined sugars, is full of nutritional goodness.

DESICCATED COCONUT is very small pieces of dried, pre-grated coconut meat. It is a very handy addition to granola, muesli and I often use it to garnish sweet treats or smoothies. Be sure to use an unsweetened variety. You can replace desiccated coconut with shredded coconut (which is more common in the USA). The difference being that shredded coconut has simply been shredded and not necessarily dried.

COCONUT FLAKES are made from dried coconut and come in big flakes. These are ideal for adding to muesli.

COCONUT OIL: I use coconut oil for baking, since it remains stable at high temperatures and has the benefit of solidifying when baked goods cool down, helping them to firm up. You can sometimes buy odourless varieties of coconut oil, which is also fine to use in baking.

Bakes & Veggie Burgers

BAKED RUSTIC SWEET POTATO FALAFELS

Makes: *12 balls*

Time: *45 mins*

Ingredients:

300g sweet potatoes
2 large cloves garlic
1 handful fresh coriander leaves
200g chickpeas (1 tin drained)
¼ teaspoon ground cardamom
2 heaped teaspoons ground coriander
1 heaped teaspoon ground cumin
2 tablespoons olive oil
1 heaped teaspoon sea salt
2 tablespoons gram flour (chickpea flour)
Extra gram flour for rolling with

Falafel was traditionally a deep-fried middle eastern dish. You can enjoy this healthy, naturally gluten-free version by baking them in the oven. Cumin and coriander are great warming spices that not only complement our health, but also add the sort of flavoursome bite that lends itself perfectly to middle eastern cuisine. Sweet potatoes bring a gorgeous soft texture to this dish, whilst adding a myriad of important nutrients (being particularly high in vitamins A and C, B vitamins, manganese and copper).

These falafels serve well hot or cold with hummus (page 64), salad or a tahini sauce (page 67).

1. Scrub and chop the sweet potato (skins on) and boil (or steam) until soft (approximately 10 minutes). Then drain and place in a mixing bowl.
2. Crush the garlic.
3. Chop the coriander leaves as small as you can with a sharp knife.
4. Put all the ingredients (except the gram flour) into a blender or food processor. I find this actually works best with a hand blender, which means you can apply downward pressure and get in there nicely… if you use a jug blender or food processor it will work fine if you keep scraping down the sides to loosen the mixture. Alternatively you could go for the real rustic effect and use a strong potato masher to do the job instead. Whatever your method, blend until most of the mixture is broken down. It doesn't need to be totally smooth - it can be quite rustic.
5. Once blended, add the gram flour and continue to thoroughly mix with a spoon. If you leave the prepared mixture on the side for a while (half an hour or half a day) then it will firm up a little, making it slightly easier to roll. If I have time, I let it stand, but that's not essential.
6. Chickpea moisture varies from batch to batch. The mixture should be soft and pliable, easy to roll into a ball in your hands. Roughly divide into 12 and roll into balls. If your mixture is too soft to roll well, add a little extra gram flour or use gram flour to roll in.
7. Place on a baking tray and bake in preheated oven at gas mark 6 or 7 (200°C/220°C) for approximately 30 minutes or until tanned.

Quinoa & Fava Bean Burgers

Makes: *6 burgers*

Time: *45 mins*

Ingredients:

100g quinoa

*120g (half a tin) fava beans
(or butter beans etc.)*

2 large cloves garlic

½ an apple

*1 very heaped tablespoon finely
chopped rosemary*

1 tablespoon dried parsley

*2 heaped teaspoons onion
powder*

4 tablespoons tomato purée

1 teaspoon apple cider vinegar

1 teaspoon sea salt

This burger just works! Not only is it tasty, it packs a powerful, easy to digest, protein punch. I originally designed this recipe with local, British grown quinoa and fava beans (also known as broad beans). Be sure to buy a fairly traded, organic quinoa (or if you are feeling really adventurous, why not grow your own). If you can't get fava beans then substitute for another type of bean like cannellini, kidney, butter beans or black-eyed beans.

1. Cook the quinoa for 20 minutes or until soft.
2. Rinse and drain half a tin of beans.
3. Crush the garlic cloves.
4. Grate the apple (with skin still on unless it's not organic).
5. Add all ingredients into a large mixing bowl and mash together thoroughly with a potato masher until everything blends together.
6. The mixture will be moist and sticky, although it should hold together really well. There is no way to avoid sticky hands at this stage, so get ready!
7. Have a plate or two ready and waiting on the kitchen counter. Shape big dollops of your burger mixture into patty shapes (up to 2cm thick) and then place them on the plate. When you have finished, you'll probably need to wash your hands before turning on the grill (or broiler if you are in the USA) to a medium heat.
8. Carefully place each patty on the wire grill tray and then slide them all under for grilling. This works best with a gas grill, although if you have an electric one, be sure that it is really hot before you put them in.
9. Keep an eye on them and when they start to tan, pull the tray out and carefully turn them over. This might be around 8 minutes each side. They should hold together beautifully if you are gentle with them. If they stick a little, just tease them off the wire and turn.
10. They serve delightfully well with my thick homemade sauces on pages 116 & 117.

Black Bean Burgers

This black bean burger recipe is an excellent, quick way to create a tasty meal. It yields scrumptious patties that can work well as an accompaniment to potato wedges, in a bap or even with rice. Firm on the outside after grilling, these burgers are also gorgeously moist on the inside, meaning that they work well with or without a sauce. If you fancy a sauce then check out my easy Homemade Ketchup (page 116) or Tomoconut Sauce (page 117).

1. You will need to use pre-cooked black beans for this recipe. So either cook up your own or buy pre-cooked in a can. If you are using the canned version, be sure to rinse and drain thoroughly before use.
2. Peel and crush the garlic and put in a mixing bowl along with the drained black beans and tomato purée.
3. Roughly mash these ingredients together. You need a rustic blend - a few whole black beans remaining along with a lot of mush is perfect. The mashed beans are going to act as a binder for this recipe.
4. Chop mushrooms into very small pieces and sauté in the olive oil for a couple of minutes.
5. Roughly chop the parsley and add to mixing bowl along with the sautéed mushrooms and all remaining ingredients.
6. Mix everything together with a spoon, pushing and pressing until everything is thoroughly combined.
7. Form patties in your hands, about 1.5cm (½inch) thick and place on a grill tray.
8. Grill for approximately 8 minutes on each side, on a medium heat.
9. Serve right away and enjoy.

Makes: *5 burgers*

Time: *25 mins*

Ingredients:

250g black beans (pre-cooked)
2 large cloves garlic
2 heaped tablespoons tomato purée
100g mushrooms
Dash of olive oil
1 handful fresh parsley
½ teaspoon ground cumin
2 teaspoons ground coriander
1 teaspoon sea salt
2 teaspoons onion granules
2 heaped tablespoons rice flour

Mushroom Chick-Peace Burgers

Makes: *4 - 6 burgers*

Time: *45 mins*

Ingredients:

2 large cloves garlic

1 small red onion

75g tasty mushrooms

240g chickpeas (about 1 tin drained weight)

½ medium-sized apple

2 level tablespoons gram flour (chickpea flour)

1 tablespoon tahini

½ teaspoon sea salt

1 tablespoon fresh rosemary (finely chopped)

1 medium-sized tomato

1 teaspoon dried parsley

This is an excellent way to enjoy a high-protein, vegan, gluten-free meal, whilst using optimal ingredients. I've created this version to be pleasantly moist on the inside with a lovely soft crisp on the outside, so that you can enjoy it with or without the addition of a sauce. It works wonders with a salad or potato wedges, or in a bap with sauce toppings…

1. Crush the garlic, dice the onion and chop the mushrooms into small pieces. Sauté together in a pan for a few minutes.
2. Roughly mash the chickpeas in a large mixing bowl with a potato masher or fork. This involves a bit of work to really get in there! The mash doesn't have to be totally smooth, although you do need to give it a good pressing so that a lot of it is quite mushy. It's fine to leave a few rustic-looking pieces.
3. Grate the half apple (including skin).
4. Add the gram flour, tahini, salt and apple, then mix all together using the back of a metal spoon (to press down and help support the binding process).
5. Finely chop the rosemary and chop the tomato into small pieces.
6. Add the sautéed items and parsley along with all the remaining ingredients into the bowl, pressing down and mixing thoroughly with a metal spoon.
7. Divide into 4 or 6, then firmly shape and mould into patties.
8. Place onto a grill tray and heat under a medium grill for approximately 8 minutes on each side (or until nicely tanned).

BEET BURGERS

Makes: 6 burgers

Time: 60 mins

Ingredients:

400g beetroots (3 medium-sized)
1 medium onion
3 large cloves garlic
Dash olive oil
200g sunflower seeds
1 handful of fresh rosemary
Small handful fresh parsley
1 tablespoon tahini
½ teaspoon sea salt

This colourful burger serves well with salad, potato wedges, rice or in a bap with Homemade Ketchup (see page 116). It involves two main stages…

1. *Baking the beetroot, onion and garlic (to soften and bring out flavour).*
2. *Mixing all ingredients together and grilling (broiling).*

The first stage is to bake the beetroot, onion and garlic in the oven until soft. I like to multi-task and bake something else at the same time so that I am making the most of the hot oven.

1. Turn oven on to gas mark 7 (220°C/425°F).
2. With skins still intact, chop the beetroot into small cubes (half inch cubes works) and place on a large baking tray
3. Remove skin from the onion, roughly chop and pop onto the tray.
4. Drizzle a dash of oil over the contents of the tray, mix the beetroot and onion about a bit and then bake for half an hour (or until you can pierce a fork through the beets). Mix the contents of the tray several times throughout baking period.
5. After about 20 minutes in the oven, toss in the 3 cloves of garlic (leaving on the skins) and allow to bake along with the beetroot and onion.
6. When baked, you need to blend the beetroot, onion and garlic together roughly, so place them in a jug to blend (pop the baked garlic out of its skin first). Pulsate a few times with your blender, until you have a rough-looking, rustic mix.
7. In the meantime, use a food processor or nut mill to grind the seeds and rosemary. You need a very rough, 'flour' consistency with quite a few rustic chunks of seeds left in. The rosemary should be finely chopped.
8. Finely chop the parsley with a sharp knife.

Bringing everything together

1. In a large mixing bowl, mix all ingredients together (including tahini and salt) using a metal spoon. Use the back of the spoon to press the ingredients, encouraging the binding process. After a minute or two, you should start to get a mixture that holds together. It is now ready to make into burgers. You can either make these now or allow the mixture to sit all day and create later.
2. Adorning hands with 'beetroot red' is a bit unavoidable at this stage. Enjoy the process! The mixture should divide nicely into six burgers. Firmly mould into burger shapes and then place on a grill tray. Grill for about 15 minutes in total, carefully turning over half way through grilling time. The outer colour should change to a lighter brown, indicating when it's time to turn over.

Quinoa Neat-Loaf

My quinoa neat-loaf is an infinitely more compassionate, high protein, plant-based version of a traditional meat-loaf. This loaf also serves well cold. I usually cook a big batch of black beans in advance for my neat-loaf and use 100g of them when cooked (the rest can either go into the freezer or go into other dishes - they will also keep in the fridge for a few days).

1. Cook the quinoa in advance. Rinse through with water in a fine-meshed sieve and then drain thoroughly.
2. Preheat the oven to gas mark 6 (200°C/400°F).
3. Grate the apple (with skin on).
4. Crush the garlic.
5. Finely chop the fresh parsley.
6. Add all ingredients together in a mixing bowl and mix.
7. Either take a hand blender and pulse roughly through the mix (pulsing about half of the mixture, leaving plenty of chunkiness) - or if you don't have a hand blender, mash down firmly with the back of a tablespoon, until everything starts sticking together (this takes a bit more effort than a hand blender so stay with it).
8. Line a loaf tin (18 x 10 x 8cm or 7 x 4 x 3inches approx) with parchment paper and then jam pack the mixture evenly inside.
9. Pop into the preheated oven.
10. After approximately 45 minutes take out, slice up and serve right away with Tomoconut Sauce (page 117) and veggies.

Serves: *4*

Time: *65 mins*

Ingredients:

150g red quinoa

1 medium apple

2 cloves garlic

Handful fresh parsley

100g black beans (pre-cooked)

½ teaspoon sea salt

1 tablespoon coconut sugar (optional)

1 teaspoon ground cumin

2 teaspoons ground coriander

Italian Basil Farinata Slice

Serves: 6

Time: *30 mins*

Ingredients:

1 medium red onion
150g chestnut mushrooms
Dash of olive or coconut oil
250g gram flour
1 teaspoon sea salt
Large pinch of black pepper
350ml water
150ml passata
75g basil (a massive handful)
3 cherry tomatoes

Farinata (also called cecina) is a traditional Italian crêpe-type slice made by creating a batter with chickpea flour, water and olive oil and baking in the oven or frying. Fresh rosemary, salt and pepper are also typically added; although my version is deliciously unique, using a generous amount of aromatic basil, mushrooms, onion and tomatoes. It's an excellent high protein, gluten-free slice. I love making up a batch of these slices before travelling on long haul flights or coach journeys. They work perfectly well cold as an alternative to sandwiches. Satiating and filling - a meal in themselves - they also serve well right out of the oven as part of a main meal, with potato wedges, veggies or salad.

1. Preheat oven to gas mark 6 (200°C/400°F).
2. Chop the onion and mushrooms into small pieces and sauté in the oil for a couple of minutes (you can actually miss this part, although a quick sauté will help to bring out the flavours).
3. Put the gram flour, salt and pepper into a large mixing bowl and gradually stir in the water to create a thick batter.
4. Mix in the passata, sautéed mushrooms and onions.
5. Chop the basil and then mix that in too.
6. Pour the mixture into a large, shallow baking tray lined with parchment paper (approximately 32 x 22cm or 12 x 9inches) - if you don't have parchment paper, simply rub a little coconut oil evenly over the tray to stop it sticking.
7. Slice and push the cherry tomatoes into the mixture when it is in the tray (see image opposite).
8. Pop it in the oven.
   Please note: baking times are slightly different depending on whether you are serving it straight out of the oven or letting it cool down before serving…

- *If you are going to let it cool down before serving then bake for about 20 minutes (it should firm up perfectly upon cooling, so be sure to let it cool before slicing).*
- *If you plan on serving it hot, right out of the oven, then it's best to let it bake slightly longer - for about 25 minutes (otherwise it might be slightly too soft and moist for slicing).*

SERIOUSLY BEETROOT CASHEW PIE

Serves: 4
Time: 80 mins
(plus soaking time)

Topping ingredients:

150g cashews

2 lemons

2 tablespoons water

½ teaspoon sea salt

1 handful fresh parsley

Extra water (to thin if needed)

Main ingredients:

4 beetroots (no larger than tennis ball size each)

1 small cauliflower

3 large garlic cloves

Heaped teaspoon grated ginger

Handful fresh parsley

200g mushrooms

125ml coconut cream

½ teaspoon sea salt

This is a colourful way to create a super nutritious pie. The coconut, garlic, mushrooms and ginger turn the beetroot into an appetising feast, whilst its vibrant burgundy colour permeates everything else. Cashew cream tops it all off with a grain-free, tangy, 'cheezy' crust. Serve with sweet potato wedges and salad.

Make the topping:

You will need to soak the cashews for the topping ahead of time. Start by juicing the lemon and allowing the cashews to soak in the lemon juice and two tablespoons of water for at least an hour. Stir a few times during this process to make sure the cashews are evenly coated. An easier option is to leave them to soak longer (or even overnight). After this time, add salt and chopped parsley then blend until creamy smooth. If the sauce is too thick, add a dash of water to achieve your desired sauce-like consistency. It should be a really thick cream - easy to spread.

Making the rest of the pie:

1. In the meantime, slice the beets and bake in the oven on gas mark 6 (200°C/400°F) until you can pierce a fork through them - this should take about 45 minutes, depending on the size that you have chopped them.
2. Divide your cauliflower into small florets and either bake until you can just pierce with a fork or alternatively, steam until almost soft.
3. Put your garlic cloves in the oven (with skins still on). After about 15 minutes they should have baked right through. Allow to cool before removing the skin.
4. Finely grate a heaped teaspoon's worth of fresh ginger.
5. Roughly chop the parsley.
6. Once the beetroot has baked, blend together with the garlic, coconut cream, fresh ginger and sea salt. The blend doesn't have to be totally smooth, as long as everything is blended together and there aren't any massive slices of beetroot in there.
7. Mix in the chopped mushrooms, cooked cauliflower and chopped parsley, then place the whole mixture into a baking dish (20cm or 8inch diameter).
8. Use the cashew sauce to create a topping.
9. Pop in the oven at gas mark 6 (200°C/400°F) and bake for about 25 minutes or until the top is nicely tanned.
10. Serve hot or cold.

Pasta & Rice Meals

Serves: *6*

Time: *20 mins*

Ingredients:

500g gluten-free pasta
500ml water (for sauce)
500g butternut squash
1 medium onion
1 large garlic clove
4 cardamom pods
1 teaspoon sea salt
1 heaped teaspoon ground coriander
100g creamed coconut block

Pasta with Cardamom Coconut Sauce

This is SUPER easy. My friends and family absolutely love this with rice pasta although it's also a winner with any sort of penne pasta or noodles. I use real cardamom pods by cracking open the pods, taking out the seeds and crushing them down to release their incredible, authentic flavour.

1. Cook pasta according to the instructions on the packet.
2. Place the 500ml of water into another pan and bring to the boil.
3. Whilst the water is coming to the boil, peel the squash (compost the skin) and chop into cubes.
4. Remove skin from onion and roughly chop.
5. Remove skin from garlic and crush.
6. Toss the squash, onion and garlic into the pan as soon as you've chopped them. Turn down to a gentle simmer once the water has come to the boil.
7. Take the seeds out of the cardamom pods. Roughly chop and crush them with a sharp knife (taking care!). Toss into the pan along with the sea salt and ground coriander.
8. Roughly chop coconut block and toss into the pan, allowing it to melt in the heat.
9. The sauce should be ready after about 15 minutes (or when the squash pierces easily with a fork).
10. Blend thoroughly with a hand blender or carefully (it's hot) pour into a jug blender and blend until creamy smooth.

CARDAMOM SEEDS

Cardamom is one of the most valued spices in the world, with an intense aromatic flavour that is used to bring out the best in both savoury and sweet dishes. It also has lots of medicinal benefits too. True cardamom (*Elettaria cardamomum*) has a green pod - this is the type that I use. You can also buy a black-podded cardamom (*Amomum costatum* and *Amomum subulatum*), which are different species that I know little about, other than they have a different, more smoky flavour. If you see white cardamom pods for sale, they are likely to be green pods that have been bleached. For vibrancy and taste I recommend green. You can easily buy cardamom powder in any store that sells herbs and spices. However, I highly recommend that you buy the actual pods rather than the ground stuff. There is a massive difference between the two. Pre-ground cardamom loses its culinary magic as the fragrant flavour disappears. I always peel open the pods, then crush the seeds with a pestle and mortar or by repeatedly chopping over them with a sharp, heavy knife.

Quinoa & Blackeyed Bean Risotto

Serves: *2*

Time: *25 mins*

Ingredients:

150g quinoa

Water for cooking quinoa

½ tin drained (120g approx) of black-eyed beans

Big handful of parsley

4 tablespoons coconut cream

1 - 2 tablespoons of tamari (or generous pinch of sea salt)

Quinoa is a small, nutty, highly nutritious, grain-like seed that has been harvested for thousands of years. I always recommend that you purchase fair trade, organic varieties and look out for locally grown quinoa. I've grown this stuff in my garden and am seeing British-grown quinoa become available over the last couple of years. This is a super easy, high-protein dish that works as a main meal or a side dish with salad.

1. Cook quinoa in water for approximately 20 minutes (you can tell when the quinoa is cooked because it starts looking more transparent and the sprout begins to separate from the seed). You'll need over three times the amount of water as you do quinoa.
2. In the meantime, drain and rinse the black-eyed beans then roughly chop the parsley.
3. A couple of minutes before the quinoa has finished cooking, add the beans (to heat them through).
4. When the quinoa (with beans added) is cooked, drain and place back in the pan on a minimum heat. Immediately stir in the coconut cream, tamari and chopped parsley. After about 30 seconds turn off the heat and serve.

Mushroom & Basil Gourmet Spaghetti Sauce

There is something about the combination of mushrooms, basil and coconut that excites my senses. The sweet richness of the coconut enriches the natural earthiness of mushrooms, whilst the basil infuses a hint of gourmet flare into the dish. This is a particularly quick-to-make pasta sauce recipe, ideal if you want something that feels both delicious and luxurious with minimal time to hand. It works well with gluten-free rice noodles, which can be cooked and ready to enjoy in a few minutes too. Be sure to select tasty mushrooms and a good quality organic coconut cream.

1. Slice or finely chop mushrooms and sauté in the olive oil for a few minutes, until the juices just begin to ooze.
2. In the meantime, mix the cornflour into the unheated coconut cream until dissolved, not adding to the pan yet.
3. Roughly chop the basil.
4. Once the mushrooms are ready, pour the coconut cream/cornflour mix into the hot pan and stir rapidly for the first few seconds to start distributing the heat evenly. Bring the contents of the pan to boiling point and continue to stir as the sauce begins to thicken with the heat.
5. As you stir, add the basil and sea salt.
6. Once boiling point has been reached, let the flavours combine by simmering and gently stirring for a couple of minutes. You don't need to continually stir, but keep watch.
7. Serve immediately with gluten-free rice noodles.

Serves: *2*

Time: *15 mins*

Ingredients:

250g chestnut mushrooms
Dash of olive oil
1 heaped teaspoon of cornflour (or use arrowroot or tapoica flour)
200ml coconut cream
30g basil
½ teaspoon sea salt

CREAMY CAULIFLOWER SAUCE - 5 WAYS

Serves: 4

Time: *25 mins*

Ingredients:

1 small cauliflower (approx 400g)

1 can (400ml) of coconut milk

4 cardamom pods

3 garlic cloves

1 teaspoon sea salt

1 heaped teaspoon ground coriander

Pinch of pepper (optional)

When most people think of creamy sauces, they usually imagine dairy milk, yoghurt or cream as an essential ingredient for a lip-lickin', smooth, buttery result. Seldom do people imagine… erm, cauliflower! Having eaten a plant-based diet for the best part of 25 years, I've developed a real passion for finding out what new dishes I can whip up from the most random vegetables. It turns out that cauliflower, especially when blended with coconut milk, comes into its element as a thick, creamy 'can't quite tell how you did that but I love it' sauce - a sauce that can be used just about anywhere that conventional cheese-type sauce would. It doesn't just work, it's absolutely fabulous! Not only is it super healthy (filled with an absolute abundance of nutritional goodness), it's ridiculously simple. Oh, and it makes a splendid soup too. On this recipe page I am sharing five different sauce suggestions. All of these recipes serve beautifully with noodles or pasta or completely on their own as a soup.

1. Chop the cauliflower and cook in a large saucepan (with lid) along with the coconut milk (no water). Bring to the boil and then turn down to a simmer.
2. Take the cardamom seeds out of the pods and chop and crush them with a knife (or pestle & mortar). Chop/crush them as finely as you can to unleash their flavour. Toss in the pan.
3. Peel and crush the garlic cloves and add to the pan along with the salt. Note: if you are using the oven at the same time for something else, roast the garlic in there to really bring out the flavour (it's not essential at all, but it does add a bit of culinary magic if you do).
4. Add the coriander and simmer for 20 minutes or until you can easily pierce the cauliflower with a fork. Then blend everything together until creamy, using a jug blender or hand blender.
5. Pour over pasta or noodles and enjoy.

Once you get going, there is no end to the ways you can use it!

Alternative version 1: "Roasted Pepper & Garlic Sauce"
Use 1 sweet pepper and 3 extra cloves of garlic.
Roast the sweet pepper and garlic in a hot oven… To do this, keep the garlic in its skin and place on an oven tray along with the pepper, then place in a preheated oven at about gas mark 7 (220°C/425°F). Roast garlic for up to 10 minutes and the pepper for about 15-20 minutes (or until the pepper is easy to pierce). No need to let the pepper char.
It's best to wait until the garlic cools down a little before you pop it out of its skin. Gently chop off the top, then squeeze out the fleshy garlic and place in a jug ready to blend with everything else.
Blend in the pepper and garlic with the original recipe then enjoy either creamy-smooth or rustic.

Alternative version 2: "Mushroom Sauce"
Sauté 200g of mushrooms and one medium-sized onion (chopped) in coconut oil, then add to the blended sauce for a chunky mushroom sauce or delicious soup.

Alternative version 3: "Scheezy Sauce"
Add two heaped tablespoons of nutritional yeast extract for a scheezy sauce.

Alternative version 4: "Super Easy Stock Cube Sauce"
Leave out the cardamom and sea salt then add a couple of gluten-free vegan stock cubes for a super easy immediate infusion of flavour.

Alternative version 5: "Totally Coconut Sauce"
Add up to 100g of creamed coconut block or up to 200g of coconut cream to the mix before blending - for a sensational infusion of coconut.

Sauce Ingredients:

600g butternut squash
(or 400g when baked)

3 large garlic cloves

100g creamed coconut block *

7 cardamom pods

350ml water

200ml passata

2 teaspoons ground coriander

1 teaspoon sea salt

Topping Ingredients:

50g sunflower seeds

50g pumpkin seeds

1 small red onion

50g brown rice flour

Sea salt to taste

3 tablespoons water

Other Ingredients:

300g red kidney beans

250g brown rice pasta

Serves: 4

Time: *90 mins*

Butternut Pasta Bake

I'd pretty much finished all the recipes for this book when I ventured out to Vancouver Island to cater on a retreat for the most beautiful group of people. When I make food, I don't always have a plan - my soul tends to guide me. This means that I never quite know what is going to happen next. During my preparation for the last meal, the only thing I could 'see' in my mind was a pasta bake. I'd never made one before, let alone make one for a group of 16 people! I couldn't visualise anything else at all - so pasta bake it was. I wanted something with a tasty creamy sauce, something filling, grounding, with a healthy crumble on top. This recipe is what happened. As soon as it was served, 'mmmmms' and 'yums' filled the room and everyone started asking for the recipe. After a few comments like 'you have to put this in the book', I went home, recreated it a few times and here we are - a very satisfying cardamom inspired, butternut, pasta bake…

Halve the squash, scoop out the seeds and pop into a preheated oven to bake at gas mark 6 (200°C/400°F), until you can easily pierce a fork through the flesh. This may take about 45 minutes. Bake your garlic cloves on the same tray for 10 minutes only. Whilst the squash is baking, prepare the rest of the sauce ingredients and topping.

Making the topping:
1. Roughly grind the seeds to create a rustic blend. I use a nut mill for this, although a food processor or pestle and mortar would work fine too, if you have time.
2. Peel and finely chop the red onion.
3. Mix the ground seeds, finely chopped onion, rice flour, salt and water together with your hands, rubbing between your fingertips to create a crumble topping.
4. Put this to the side whilst you make the rest of your bake.

Making the sauce and cooking the pasta:
1. Roughly chop the coconut block and place in a medium-sized pan.
2. Crush the seeds from the cardamom pods using a pestle and mortar (discard outer pods).
3. Add the water, passata, coriander, sea salt and cardamom to the pan.
4. When the squash and garlic have baked, you might find it easier to let them cool down a little. They are easier to handle that way. Scoop out all of the squash into the pan.
5. Cut the end off each baked garlic clove and remove the outer skin, before putting into the pan.
6. Bring the pan to the boil and then cook on a low heat for around 15 minutes to allow the creamed coconut to melt, the tomato (passata) to 'soften' and the flavours to infuse.
7. In the meantime, cook the rice pasta according to the packet instructions. It is ready when it is 'just' cooked. Be careful not to overcook the pasta. Rinse through with cold water and thoroughly drain.
8. Back to the sauce: once cooked through, blend the sauce until creamy smooth.

Bringing the bake together:
1. Mix the beans and pasta (do not blend these in) into the sauce. Place this mixture into a baking dish (approximately 21 x 21 x 5cm or 10 x 10 x 2inches) and evenly apply the topping.
2. Place the dish into a preheated oven at gas mark 6 (200°C/400°F) and bake until the topping is gently tanned. This should take around 25 minutes.
3. Enjoy with a healthy raw salad. It also serves beautifully cold, if you happen to have any left over.

* Note: this works best with creamed coconut (the type that comes as a solid block). This adds to the lush creaminess. If you can't get hold of creamed coconut, then you could try 300ml of coconut cream instead (whilst omitting most of the water from the ingredient list). Coconut cream is like a pouring cream and won't thicken the sauce like the creamed coconut block does, so if you play with the ingredients, be sure to take out most of the water.

Black Bean Bolognese
with warming spices

Serves: *3*

Time: *20 mins*

Ingredients:

7 cardamom pods

1 heaped teaspoon grated ginger

Handful fresh parsley

100g creamed coconut block

250g tasty mushrooms

Dash of coconut oil

480g cooked black beans (equivalent to 2 cans drained)

700g passata

1 teaspoon sea salt

½ teaspoon black pepper

I just adore this good old hearty, black bean alternative to the traditional Italian bolognese sauce. It makes use of warming spices like ginger, cardamom and black pepper, whilst embracing the gift of creamed coconut for a uniquely extravagant, international variation. This serves particularly well with brown rice, perfect yellow rice (page 113) or noodles.

1. Take the cardamom seeds out of the pods and either grind them down with a pestle and mortar, or chop as finely as you can by going over and over them with a sharp heavy knife. This is essential to unleash their divine flavour with such a short cooking time.
2. Peel and grate a generous heaped teaspoon's worth of fresh ginger.
3. Roughly chop the parsley.
4. Roughly chop the creamed coconut block.
5. Slice and chop the mushrooms.
6. Use a medium-sized pan to melt the coconut oil (if solid), turn up the heat and sauté the chopped mushrooms for a few minutes (or until cooked through and just starting to release their earthy juices).
7. Once the mushrooms are cooked, toss in all other ingredients and bring to the boil. Stir frequently and then cook until the creamed coconut block has melted in. Leave on a low heat for up to ten minutes to allow the flavours to infuse together.
8. Alternatively, turn off when the coconut has melted in. Leave a lid on and reheat again later when you are ready to use. If you prefer, you can leave out the fresh parsley until the end and toss it in a couple of minutes before serving.
9. This reheats well if you don't use it all in one go, keeping for a few days in the fridge.

Tasty Sides

Mint Potato Patties

Serves: 6

Time: *35 mins*

Ingredients:

3 large potatoes
50g creamed coconut block
1 teaspoon sea salt
Handful fresh mint

This is a tasty way to create a minty potato side addition to a meal. It's also an excellent use for leftover potatoes (adjust the ingredients accordingly). Not only do they make a fabulous hot or cold accompaniment to a salad, they will work pretty much anywhere you'd normally serve potatoes.

1. Scrub potatoes and chop into small chunks with the skins still on.
2. Boil for about 10 minutes (or until you can pierce them easily with a fork).
3. Finely chop the coconut block and put to the side.
4. Drain potatoes thoroughly, straining out as much water as possible.
5. Place the potatoes back into the pan, mix in the chopped coconut and replace the lid.
6. Once the coconut has melted, add the salt and mash together thoroughly with a potato masher.
7. Finely chop the mint leaves and mix into the potatoes with a spoon.
8. If you have the time, allow the mixture to cool and stiffen before creating patties.
9. When ready, divide evenly into about 6 and firmly shape into patties with your hands. Place onto a grill tray and then grill on a medium heat for about 7 minutes on each side (or until nicely tanned). They should hold together well, although you will need to take care when turning them over in the grill.

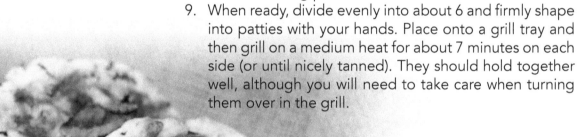

Perfect Yellow Rice

Cooking long grain brown rice didn't used to be my forte. It's hardly surprising that so many people struggle with rice when the packet instructions tend to tell us to simply boil it for about 40 - 50 minutes, which so often makes it soggy and clumpy. I admit, I've had my fair share of half-hearted rice disasters over the years! Then one day I decided to make peace with this useful grain and learned that in fact, it's best to cook it for half an hour, strain it, rinse it in hot water, and then pop back in the hot pan, allowing to cook using the warmth in the pan for a final ten minutes. Different types of rice have different cooking times, although you can use the same sort of principle for all of them. You'll notice that I've included cups to measure this recipe with, which makes it so simple. You can use a standard measuring cup or any old cup from the cupboard as long as the rice water ratio is about 1:3.

I like to add turmeric for its health benefits and vibrant colour; but bear in mind that you can cook rice just the same without it.

Serves: *2*

Time: *40 mins*

Ingredients:

1 cup (180g) of long grain brown rice
3 cups (750ml) of water or more
1 level teaspoon of ground turmeric
½ teaspoon sea salt

1. Using a large pan with a well fitting lid, bring 3 cups of water to the boil. It is better to have too much water than too little - that way you don't run the risk of having it boil dry and burning the rice.
2. Add the rice, turmeric and sea salt then simmer on the lowest heat for 30 minutes.
3. When the time is nearly up, boil a kettle with about 2 cups (500ml) of water. Drain the rice in a fine-meshed strainer and rinse with the kettle of hot water. This should remove any remaining starchiness from around the rice and stop it clumping together.
4. Shake off the water and put the strained rice back into the hot pan (which should have now been removed from the heat source). Replace the lid (which is why a tight-fitting lid is ideal) and allow to cook in its own heat for a further 10 minutes. A little longer is fine too, if the rest of your meal is still cooking. This final 'resting' period allows the rice to continue to cook in the warmth of the pan, whilst making sure it stays firm and doesn't go soggy.
5. When ready, remove the lid and fluff up with a fork. The rice should be firm, yet soft.
6. Serve warm alongside a main meal or allow to cool and use as part of a rice salad.

Sweet Potato Wedges

The first time I ever had sweet potato wedges was in a London pub many moons ago. At the time, I had finished running a weekend workshop and was looking everywhere for a decent menu at the end of a long day. It wasn't looking promising, until this place with a healthy-looking menu caught my eye. I apprehensively ordered sweet potato wedges and salad, not quite knowing what to expect. To my surprise, I couldn't believe how delicious they have been in love with them ever since.

Botanically speaking, sweet potatoes are totally unrelated to regular white potatoes. They are quite a bit lower on the glycemic index, making them a great alternative if you are watching your blood sugar levels. Sweet potatoes also contain the highest source of vitamin A and beta carotene in any known root vegetable! This is an easy recipe involving very little effort. Just slice, coat and pop them in the oven whilst you get on with the rest of dinner.

Serves: *2*

Time: *40 mins*

Ingredients:

1 tablespoon fresh rosemary
1 tablespoon olive oil
½ teaspoon celtic sea salt
2 medium to large organic sweet potatoes

1. Preheat the oven to gas mark 7 (220°C/425°F).
2. Finely chop a tablespoon's worth of fresh rosemary.
3. Mix the olive oil, rosemary and sea salt together.
4. Scrub the sweet potatoes clean and then chop into thick wedge shapes, skins still on.
5. Mix the olive oil blend with the wedges in a mixing bowl, using your hands to make sure that the wedges are evenly coated.
6. Place in your preheated oven on a high shelf and bake for approximately 35 minutes. They should be soft on the inside and a little crispy or tanned on the outside. Turn over the wedges half way through the cooking period.
7. Serve hot as a side dish.

Kale & Mushroom Side

The beauty of this dish (apart from the delectable taste) is that it only takes 5 minutes to make. This is exactly the sort of thing I create when arriving home late and want to have something ready in a flash. The kale and mushrooms shrink right down, so you need a decent volume of these things, making it a nutrient-rich side dish. It works well on pasta, on toast, with potatoes, wedges or even as a quick, warm lunch bowl on its own.

1. Finely chop the kale into bite-sized slices.
2. Crush the garlic.
3. Slice the mushrooms.
4. Heat a splash of olive oil in a large pan and turn up to a high heat.
5. When hot, toss in the mushrooms, stir, then toss in the garlic.
6. Sauté for a couple of minutes, until the mushrooms begin to change colour and shrink down a little.
7. Put three tablespoons of water in before tossing in the sliced kale leaves.
8. Add the coconut cream and mix in thoroughly.
9. Cook for a few minutes. Stir a few times, replacing the lid each time. Cook until the kale has wilted right down, yet still retains its green vibrancy.
10. Serve immediately as a side dish along with a main meal or enjoy as a light lunch.

Serves: *2 - 3*

Time: *5 mins*

Ingredients:

10 large kale leaves
2 large garlic cloves
200g tasty brown mushrooms
Splash of olive oil
3 tablespoons water
6 tablespoons thick coconut cream

TANGY GINGER SAUCE with ketchup option

Sometimes a recipe just needs a sauce. If you are going to great lengths to make sure that everything you eat is healthy, then why not enjoy a rich, tasty, healthy sauce too. Shop-bought sauces are often full of stuff we really don't want to be putting in our bodies. This one is infused with fresh ginger and coriander leaves. I use coconut cream for creaminess, tomato for tang, and arrowroot powder to thicken. It works either fresh from the stove as a thick pouring sauce over veggie burgers or wedges; or if you let it cool down, it turns into a super healthy, fresh ketchup alternative.

Time: 7 *mins*

Ingredients:

50ml rice milk (or other plant milk)
2 teaspoons arrowroot powder
1 teaspoon fresh ginger
100ml organic coconut cream
1 teaspoon brown rice vinegar
½ teaspoon sea salt
1 tablespoon tomato purée
1 teaspoon maple syrup
Small handful of coriander leaves

1. Dissolve the arrowroot powder into the cold rice milk by stirring with a spoon.
2. Peel and grate a teaspoonful of fresh ginger.
3. Put all ingredients into a small saucepan.
4. Bring to the boil, being careful to stir well as the sauce begins to thicken. This should only take a couple of minutes once it is hot.
5. The arrowroot powder acts as a thickening agent, so this should rapidly thicken with heat. If it is too thick for you, gradually add a little more coconut cream or rice milk to achieve desired consistency.
6. Serve fresh or allow to cool (and thicken) and use as a super healthy, ginger ketchup alternative.

Anastasia's Original Tomoconut Sauce

This has got to be my all time favourite sauce, using my signature combination of tomatoes and coconut. When I first created this recipe the culinary alchemy inspired such an amazing feeling I cried out *"Oh my God, this is the best tomato sauce in the world!"*. When it all clicked together I just knew I'd found something magical.

It's ideal to use with veggie burgers, potato wedges, or as a base for pasta or soup. It's very versatile and ridiculously simple to make too. It works best with creamed coconut block (which comes in solid form) or coconut butter (be careful not to confuse this with coconut oil). This adds a luxurious depth to the sauce with a melt-in-the-mouth infusion of coconut flavour and an impressive, natural creaminess (see page 82 for more about different forms of coconut).

Time: *10 mins*

Ingredients:

50g creamed coconut block (or coconut butter)

150ml passata

1 tablespoon tamari

1 tablespoon apple cider vinegar

1 large garlic clove

1 teaspoon grated ginger

1 small handful of fresh parsley

1. Chop up your coconut block and place in a saucepan along with the passata, tamari and apple cider vinegar. Turn on the heat to allow the coconut to melt and the flavours to start to infuse.
2. Crush the garlic, finely grate the ginger and toss into the saucepan.
3. Finely chop the parsley and mix it in.
4. Give the sauce a few minutes to cook to allow all the flavours to dance together. Serve hot or cold as desired.

Gluten-Free Sunshine Loaf

Makes: *1 loaf*

Time: *50 mins*

Ingredients:
100g buckwheat flakes
100g rice flour
100g ground sunflower seeds
5 tablespoons ground flaxseeds
3 tablespoon tapioca flour
1 heaped tablespoon dried herbs
Pinch sea salt (to taste)
2 tablespoons coconut oil
250ml water

When I went gluten-free, bread was the one thing that I really missed. Nothing compares to a thick, hearty piece of bread. My initial efforts weren't particularly successful, until one day I felt this new inspiration bubbling up from within, that led me to use a few ingredients that I had in my kitchen. It worked like magic. This loaf was the result. It holds together really well and is very filling, with a very welcoming, nutrient-rich density.

1. Turn on the oven to gas mark 6 (200°C/400°F).
2. Mix all ingredients in a large bowl until combined.
3. Line a loaf tin (18 x 10 x 8cm or 9 x 4 x 3inches approx) with parchment paper and then jam-pack the mixture evenly inside.
4. Pop in the oven for about 45 minutes.
5. Take out and either allow to cool or slice and serve right out of the oven.
6. This keeps for up to a week in the fridge.

Rice & Flax Flat Bread

This easy recipe is designed to serve as a side with soup or salad dips. It's loaded with flax and sunflower seeds, so you can be sure that you are filling up on healthy nutrients, at the same time as feeling satiated. It works well to dunk this flat bread into homemade hummus or serve it alongside one of my tomato based soups. It works best warm, right out of the oven, although you can also enjoy it once it has cooled down or even toasted under the grill.

1. Preheat your oven to gas mark 6 (200°C/400°F) and line a shallow baking tray (minimum size 20 x 20cm or 8 x 8 inches) with parchment paper.
2. Mix all the dry ingredients together thoroughly in a mixing bowl and then add the wet ingredients.
3. Mix everything together with a spoon until you start to form a dough. Use the back of your spoon to press the ingredients or use your hands if you prefer (in fact hands are the easiest way to get it all to bind).
4. Press and work the mixture down on the parchment paper to form a layer approximately ½cm (¼inch) thick (a little thicker works fine too). You might not fill the entire baking tray, in which case you'll need to form the edges of the flat bread using your fingers.
5. Use a sharp knife to score the flat bread into triangles.
6. Place into a preheated oven and bake for approximately 20 minutes.
7. Serve immediately, right out of the oven.

Makes: *10 triangles*

Time: *30 mins*

Ingredients:

100g rice flour

40g potato flour (or coconut flour)

4 tablespoons sunflower seed (ground)

4 tablespoons ground flaxseed

½ teaspoon celtic sea salt

1 tablespoon tomato purée

125ml water

Easy Berry Chia Jam

Makes: *1 jar*

Time: *35 mins*

Ingredients:

½ lemon

3 tablespoons chia seeds

½ teaspoon vanilla extract

300g fresh strawberries or raspberries

A teaspoon (or so) of coconut sugar (optional)

I have fond childhood memories of my mother's jam. She used to make jams and jellies out of whatever fruits were in abundance at the time. They tasted awesome, although I must admit they took ages to make with lots of boiling and precision required. This is an amazing, fresh, super-food alternative that is quick to create. It's free from refined sugar whilst benefiting from the jelly-like properties of chia seeds.

1. Juice your lemon, discarding the rind. Pour the juice into a blending jug along with the chia seeds and vanilla extract.
2. Remove any green leaves from your strawberries/raspberries and add the berries to the jug.
3. Blend until everything has evenly combined together. I use a hand blender for this and it takes about 10 seconds.
4. If it needs a little extra sweetener, blend in the coconut sugar at this stage, to your desired taste.
5. Pop the blended mix into the fridge, allowing the ingredients to infuse together. The chia seeds will help to create a gorgeous jelly-like consistency in less than half an hour.
6. Serve fresh with dessert, breakfast, as a spread on a cracker or right off the spoon.
7. This keeps in the fridge for about a week.

MAKING FOOD FROM THE HEART

Being in the kitchen is like a meditation to me. Not in the traditional sense, of course… it's not like I am sitting in a lotus pose on my counter or anything! It's more like a moving dance as I feel inspired from one ingredient to the next, having fun in the kitchen. What better kind of meditation is there?

A person's state of consciousness makes a big difference to the final outcome of a dish. If we feel 'light' and spacious within, then we essentially infuse 'light' into the food. It becomes a profound expression of our soul. You'll probably already recognise that being happy in the kitchen, mysteriously makes your food taste delicious. If you simply set off with the feeling that you are 'making your food from the heart', then it all just works.

Raw & No-bake
Sweet Treats

Raw Hazelnut Chocolate Covered Slice

Serves: 6
Time: *20 mins*
(plus soaking and chilling)

Ingredients:

50g hazelnuts (soak)
50g almonds (soak)
100g dates (don't soak)
2 heaped tablespoons tahini
2 tablespoons desiccated coconut
1 teaspoon vanilla extract

Topping Ingredients:

4 tablespoons coconut oil
2 teaspoons coconut sugar
2 tablespoons cacao powder (or lucuma powder)
½ teaspoon vanilla extract (if using cacao)
Extra few hazelnuts (optional)

The no-bake element of this hazelnut slice makes it a very appealing, nutrient-dense dessert. I normally use a food processor to create this, although a blender will also work (with a slightly different outcome - see note below). Apart from the soaking and chilling, the actual time that you spend making this is surprisingly short. You'll find that if you use good quality ingredients, it will yield the most scrumptious results. If you prefer a no-chocolate alternative then simply replace the cacao powder with lucuma powder and only use 1 teaspoon of coconut sugar.

1. Ahead of time soak the hazelnuts and almonds in water for approximately 3 hours.
2. When ready, strain and rinse the water off the nuts.
3. Place nuts in a food processor along with the dates, tahini, coconut and vanilla extract then blend until the whole mixture begins to combine together. This should be a mixture of very small chunks that hold together nicely upon compression. Take off the lid, scrape down the sides and blend further until you achieve the consistency you are looking for.
4. Line a loaf tin with parchment paper, then press in the mixture evenly and firmly. Pop into the fridge whilst you make the cacao topping.

To make the topping:

1. Roughly crush or chop the extra hazelnuts with a sharp, heavy knife (if you are opting to garnish).
2. Gently turn your coconut oil to liquid (if it is solid), and mix in the coconut sugar, cacao powder and vanilla extract. Pour this on top of the pressed slice and immediately sprinkle on the hazelnuts before the chocolate sets. Pop the loaf tin straight into the fridge to chill before serving.
3. When ready, use a sharp knife to slice into bars.

Note: If you don't have a food processor then try blending this or milling the nuts instead - although it will have a slightly different outcome. First chop the dates as finely as you can and then blend with the nuts (after soaking) but don't over blend. Mix in the tahini and desiccated coconut by hand using a metal spoon (a downward pressing motion with the back of spoon will help).

Raw Raspberry Coconut Bars

Fresh raspberries work delightfully well in desserts, especially with a chocolate-topped no-bake sweet treat. This is a truly bountiful feast that also happens to freeze really well. So if you have a special occasion coming up, you can take it all in your stride by preparing these well in advance and then forget about them. Although, admittedly, it's difficult to forget about these once you know you have a batch right there waiting in your freezer! Watch out for hungry midnight-feasters because once the word gets out about how delicious they taste… your precious batch will quickly disappear. As with all soft fruits, be extra sure to buy organic to keep you and your friends super healthy.

You will need to prepare ahead of time by soaking the dates for the filling for 1 hour and the base layer dates and raisins for 20 minutes.

Base layer:

1. Soak dates and raisins for 20 minutes.
2. Grind brazil nuts and walnuts in food processor for about 30 seconds, to start breaking them down. It's fine if they are still rather chunky.
3. Add the vanilla extract, soaked dates and raisins (taking care not to add the dates that you are soaking for the filling by mistake!). Process for about 30 seconds or until it looks very roughly blended together. I say roughly, because the base works well if it still has lots of chunks in it. If it starts sticking together between your fingers then it's perfect.
4. Line a dish (approx 18 x 13cm/7 x 5inches) with parchment paper and spread the mixture evenly. Press down very firmly to create a solid base layer. Pop into the freezer to chill whilst creating the filling.

Raspberry filling:

1. After soaking the dates for about an hour, drain and place into a jug with the raspberries, coconut oil (this may be more buttery than liquid - which is fine) and vanilla extract. Blend roughly with a hand blender or food processor by pulsing a few times.
2. Add the ground almonds and desiccated coconut and pulse a few more times.
3. Spoon your raspberry filling on top of the base layer. Press down and spread evenly across dish.
4. Place in the freezer again to chill whilst making (or melting) the chocolate topping. Note: the chocolate pours onto the filling best after the filling has been chilled, allowing it to set quickly. However, if it is too cold, the chocolate sets instantly, making it trickier to garnish with the raspberries and desiccated coconut, so try to find a happy balance.
5. Slice remaining raspberries, ready to garnish.
6. Pour chocolate on top, tilting and tipping the dish to encourage it to spread evenly. Quickly sprinkle coconut on top of the chocolate before it sets hard. Push down your raspberries into the chocolate to decorate.
7. Pop your finished dish into the fridge or freezer to set before slicing and serving.

Makes: *10 slices*
Time: *45 mins*
(plus soaking)

Base Ingredients:

75g dates
75g raisins
100g brazil nuts
50g walnuts
1 teaspoon vanilla extract

Filling:

100g dates
75g fresh raspberries
25g raw coconut oil
¼ teaspoon vanilla extract
50g ground almonds
50g desiccated coconut

Topping:

75g raw homemade chocolate (see page 140)
Sprinkle of desiccated coconut
25g extra raspberries

Makes: *8 -10 slices*

Time: *25 mins*

(plus soaking)

Cake Ingredients:

200g dates

200g walnuts

2 large carrots

½ teaspoon nutmeg (freshly ground)

1 teaspoon fresh ginger (grated)

2 teaspoons ground cinnamon

2 tablespoons coconut oil (not melted)

6 tablespoons ground almonds

Cream Frosting Ingredients:

Large handful cashews

Large handful dates

Dash of vanilla extract

Desiccated coconut to decorate

NO-BAKE CARROT CAKE

This is one of the very first recipes I created right at the beginning of my culinary journey. The no-bake carrot cake is special to me and it's a real joy to share it with you. It's best to use a food processor to get the right cake-like consistency; although you can get away with using a blender or even a hand blender (but beware that you don't over blend it!).

I use soaked dates, walnuts and carrots to create the main body of the cake, along with a delectable dance of flavours from freshly ground nutmeg, fresh ginger and ground cinnamon. Every ingredient is full of goodness. In fact each slice of cake is a meal in itself!

Soak the following ingredients in pure water (to make them easy to blend later)…

- The dates (for the cake) - for about 2 hours.
- The cashew and dates (for the creamy frosting) for at least 2 hours (you can leave the frosting ingredients soaking for a lot longer).

How to make the cake:
1. After 2 hours soaking, drain the dates for the cake. Put into to the food processor with the walnuts and process for about 20 seconds, until you get a rustic chunkiness. It should not be a purée, although it should easily stick together.
2. Grate carrot and add to food processor.
3. Grate nutmeg and ginger with a fine grater then add to the processor along with the ground cinnamon.
4. Add 1 tablespoon of coconut oil. Note: coconut oil actually only turns to oil at 24°C (76°F), so unless you live in a really warm place, it's probably solid (a soft kind of solid). That's perfect.
5. Combine all ingredients (except ground almonds) in the food processor, pulsing, taking off the lid and scraping down as required. It shouldn't take long to blend all ingredients together. A chunky rustic blend is required - where everything is chopped up small, but holding together when pressed.
6. Place mixture into a mixing bowl. Add ground almonds and mix everything together using a pressing motion with the back of a metal spoon. If you see any solid lumps of coconut oil, just work and press them in until they disappear.
7. Scrape ingredients onto a large plate and mould into a shape of choice (square, round, heart, star - whatever you like). Place in the fridge for as little or as long as you want to.

To make the creamy frosting:
1. Soak the cashews and dates for at least 2 hours to make them soft enough to blend. This is a minimum soak time. You can leave them for a lot longer (even overnight) if you prefer. Once soaked, drain thoroughly, add a dash of vanilla extract and blend until you achieve a thick cream.
2. Spread frosting evenly and thickly over the cake.
3. Serve as it is or sprinkle with coconut and garnish with walnuts or edible flowers etc.

This cake will keep in the fridge for a few days or can be served immediately. It should taste great as it is, although the flavours will continue to dance and entwine with time.

Variation note: This cake is wonderfully forgiving if you vary the ingredients. For example, if you don't have coconut oil you can totally leave it out, or if you prefer you can substitute the ground almonds for ground sunflower seeds (etc.) and still get an amazing cake. You can add a little more or less of the warming spices too, depending on personal taste.

Lucuma Melting Moments

Lucuma is a special plant that happily grows in South America. It's considered to be a superfood by some and, like many plant foods, with lots of nutrients it certainly does lend itself to health and wellness. The reason I love it so much however, is that it gives a naturally delicious caramel sort of taste, turning desserts into a sensual, heavenly experience. Like most superfoods, it's fairly pricey to buy (which is actually a good thing, because it means that there is much more of a chance that growers in South America will get a fairer deal for their crop). I buy it in powdered form, every once in a while as a treat.

1. 'Shave' the solid cacao butter with a sharp knife or grater. Shaving is just really thin slicing that makes the cacao butter crumble. You can leave it in big chunks if you like, but be prepared to wait a while for it to melt.
2. Melt the cacao butter. You can do this by leaving it in a warm place in a heat-proof glass bowl by a fire or directly above a hot radiator. It melts at 34°C. If you don't have a gentle heat source then use a hob/stove. Put the cacao butter in a small, oven proof, glass bowl and then put that bowl in a pan containing an inch or two of really hot water. Keep the hob/stove on a low heat. The heat will transfer through the bowl, melting the cacao butter.
3. Once melted, mix in the lucuma powder, coconut and raisins, then scoop into a chocolate making mould. Note: if you don't have a chocolate mould you can either line a small container with parchment paper, pour in the mixture and make a bar instead or pour it directly into a used flexible plastic container (like a used hummus pot). Instead of having neatly formed shapes, you can break it up into rustic chunks.
4. Pop your container in the fridge or freezer to chill. This should take about 15 minutes in the freezer or half an hour in the fridge. When solid, your Lucuma Melting Moments should pop out easily. They will keep for a few weeks if refrigerated (longer if frozen).

Makes: *8 hearts*

Time: *25 mins*

Ingredients:

60g raw cacao butter

4 tablespoons lucuma powder

2 heaped tablespoons desiccated coconut

50g raisins

Food prepared from the heart, using healthy, plant-based ingredients not only nurtures your mind, body and spirit, it begins to send healing ripples through the world around us, literally making the world a better place.

Easy Chocolate Truffles

Who doesn't love simple, quick recipes that not only taste divine, but are made with very few ingredients? This is one of my timeless favourites - a recipe that I have tried and tested in many different forms for the best part of 25 years (how time flies when you are having fun in the kitchen!). Not only is it absolutely delicious, it requires no baking. As with all of my recipes this has no dairy, no refined sugar and is made with the biggest heartful of love. The recipe itself is super quick to make (although you do need to remember to soak the nuts and dates ahead of time). It has always been a real winner with just about everyone I know.

Makes: *5 -10 balls*
Time: *10 mins*
(plus 3 hours soaking)

Ingredients:
100g almonds (raw or blanched)
100g dates (pitted)
1 teaspoon vanilla extract
2 tablespoons cacao powder
2 tablespoons desiccated coconut

1. Soak almonds and dates in water for about 3 hours, using enough water to rise a few centimetres above them. This will soften them to make the blending process easier.
2. After 3 hours, thoroughly drain the dates and almonds (soaking for any longer will probably make them go a little too soft). Place in a food processor along with the vanilla extract and blend until they start to bind together. This mixture doesn't have to be super smooth, although it works best if the pieces are really small and are starting to stick together.
3. Add the cacao powder and mix in until evenly spread throughout.
4. Roll into small balls in your hands, and then roll the balls in the desiccated coconut to evenly coat and finish off.
5. Enjoy fresh, just as they are - or pop into a container and store in the fridge (they'll keep for at least a week).

Simple Variations
Nuts: this recipe works well with cashews, walnuts or pecans too. Although you don't need to soak these ones (unlike the almonds) as they have a natural 'blendable' softness anyway.
Cacao: try carob or lucuma powder as a cacao alternative.
Coconut alternative: try rolling in sesame seeds or ground almonds instead.

Coconut Chocolate Fudge

This is a super easy recipe. Creamed coconut block or coconut butter (not to be confused with coconut cream or coconut oil - see page 82 for more about the different types of coconut products) makes the perfect base for this 'fudge'. If you are able to find the blocks of creamed coconut in your health food store, they will be a lot cheaper than coconut butter (which is essentially the same thing just packaged differently). This recipe delivers an unbelievable sweet, fudgey, coconut bite, followed by a delicate sweet-bitter hit of chocolate. With only 4 ingredients, it proves that delectable deliciousness doesn't have to be complicated and time consuming. You can whip this up in a few minutes before popping it into the freezer to set.

Makes: *12 fudge squares*
Time: *35 mins*

Ingredients:

*100g coconut butter
(or creamed coconut block)*

3 tablespoons maple syrup

2 tablespoons cacao powder

1 teaspoon vanilla extract

Desiccated coconut to sprinkle

1. Chop and melt the coconut butter/creamed coconut block in a small saucepan. This should melt as soon as it starts to get warm. Be careful not to burn the coconut to the pan. You just need to heat it enough to melt it.
2. Once melted, immediately take off the heat and mix in the other ingredients.
3. Scoop into a small parchment lined container (approximately 10 x 10cm/4 x 4inches in size), smooth down evenly and sprinkle on the desiccated coconut if desired.
4. Pop into the freezer for about a half an hour.
5. Chop into small cubes and pop in the fridge until you're ready to serve.
Note: you can also store this in the freezer (it works as as a very firm fudge from frozen).

Buddha Bites

Makes: *10 balls*
Time: *5 mins*

Ingredients:
100g walnuts
2 tablespoons ground flaxseeds
2 teaspoon hemp protein powder
2 teaspoon ground chia seeds
4 teaspoons raw cacao powder
4 teaspoons maple syrup
1 teaspoon vanilla extract
1 teaspoon ground cinnamon

The simplicity and ease with which we can make these super-food bites, means that high vibrational treats can be forever at your fingertips. Not only are they brimming with some of nature's most nutrient-rich superfoods, they only take five minutes to make! The addition of hemp protein powder and chia seeds makes them high in protein, whilst essential fatty acids are abundant thanks to the flax, walnut and (again) chia seeds. Raw cacao is a well-known mood elevator, whilst the whole-lot together is bursting with soul-lifting goodness. They are soft and sweet with a gentle crunch.

1. Crush the walnuts with a pestle and mortar, a rolling pin or grind them in a nut mill.
2. Mix all ingredients together, using a downward pressing motion with the back of a metal spoon to combine and bind everything together thoroughly. The ingredients should hold together well once the mixture has been thoroughly pressed.
3. Roll into heaped teaspoon-sized balls. Use a little extra cacao powder to roll and coat with if you prefer.

ABOUT FLAXSEEDS

Flaxseeds are a high fibre seed that make a frequent appearance in my recipes. It is difficult to digest whole flaxseed, so I always grind mine down with my nut mill. You can also buy it pre-ground. It makes an excellent addition to a smoothie or breakfast sprinkle.

Flaxseed is the top plant-based source of omega-3 essential fatty acid. It also contains up to a whopping 800 times more lignans than any other plant food. Lignans are not only known for their antioxidant properties, they are also a phytoestrogen, making them very supportive for hormone health and the menopause. Numerous studies have also shown that ground and whole flaxseeds remain remark-ably stable when baked and therefore make a great addition to pastries and cakes. Flax oil makes a great salad dressing ingredient, although (unlike the actual seeds), the oil should never be heated.

Cardamom Spiced Raw Mango Pie

Cardamom is a sweet spice that works well in both sweet and savoury dishes. In this recipe I use the freshly crushed seeds from the pods to create a lavish outburst of flavour, that gently melts through the whole raw pie experience. This pie requires no heating at all, ensuring that the vibrancy of the fresh ingredients is at its finest.

Base/crust:

1. Soak the dates and raisins in pure water for 30 minutes and then thoroughly drain (be careful not to let them get too soft). If the dates are particularly tough then chop them before soaking.
2. Crack open your cardamom pods then finely chop the seeds over and over with a sharp, heavy knife (or crush with a pestle and mortar) to unleash their flavour.
3. Place the walnuts into a food processor and give them a quick whiz to roughly chop them (don't overdo it).
4. Add the dates and raisins to the food processor and process until they begin to stick together. The dried fruits should be largely broken down, with some smaller chunks remaining.
5. Mix in the ground flaxseeds, vanilla extract and chopped cardamom seeds with a spoon, pressing downwards with the spoon to help everything combine nicely together.
6. Line a dish or round baking tin (about 20cm/8inch diameter) with parchment paper and then firmly press the mixture into the dish, until it is even all around. Pop your base into the fridge while you prepare the topping.

Topping:

1. Peel and chop the mango.
2. Blend the mango with the vanilla extract and coconut oil.
3. Then blend in the ground flaxseeds.
4. Mix the desiccated coconut in by hand.
5. Scrape the mixture on top of the base layer. Pop the whole thing in the freezer for about an hour before serving. Freezing helps the ingredients to thicken up and makes it much easier to take out of the dish.
6. Once it has been in the freezer for a while, you can take it out and leave it in the fridge until you are ready to serve.
7. This always serves best chilled.

Serves: 6
Time: *25 mins*
(plus soaking and freezing)

Base/Crust Ingredients:

100g dates
50g raisins
2 cardamom pods
100g walnuts
1 heaped tablespoon ground flaxseeds
½ teaspoon vanilla extract

Topping Ingredients:

1 medium-sized ripe mango
½ teaspoon vanilla extract
1 heaped tablespoon semi-solid coconut oil
1 heaped tablespoon ground flaxseeds
50g desiccated coconut

Mango Coconut Cream
with Ice Cream Option

When exquisite sweet treats are this easy to make, I really do have to pinch myself. Remarkably, this involves only two ingredients and minimal preparation time. Be sure to use the best quality organic coconut milk for optimal results. It can be enjoyed in several different ways...

- As a thick creamy mango pudding eaten right off the spoon.
- As a delicious pouring sauce over cakes and puddings.
- As part of a parfait dessert with layers of mango cream, ice cream, fresh fruits and chia pudding.
- At breakfast time it can be used in the same way that you might use yoghurt - poured over fresh fruit and sprinkled with granola.
- It makes an awesome ice cream too. No ice cream maker required; just a freezer and a little waiting time for it to slightly thaw and be creamed up again.
- OK... one more. If you have lolly moulds or containers, this makes an excellent summer time ice lolly too!

Right, let's get started...

Serves: *2 - 4*
Time: *5 mins*
(plus soaking and freezing)

Ingredients:
75g sun-dried organic mango
400ml full-fat tinned organic coconut milk

1. Soak the sun-dried mango in the coconut milk overnight, or for at least 3 hours. This is to soften the sun-dried mango before blending.
2. When ready, blend until creamy smooth.
3. Store in a glass jar or serve immediately.

Mango Coconut Ice Cream Option

If you would like to turn this into ice cream, then spread onto a tray. To make it quickly, spread on a large tray, place in the freezer and then let it freeze for an hour. If you use a smaller, deeper container, the freeze time will be longer. Take it out of the freezer and let it gently adjust to the warmth of the room for about 15 minutes (assuming you've used a large, shallow tray - if you've used a small, deep container, the thaw time will be longer). Scoop the frozen mango/coconut blend into a big bowl and then cream up by using a downward pressing motion with the back of a metal spoon (or use a hand blender). It should be soft and creamy. Serve immediately.

Easy Homemade Raw Chocolate

Makes: *1 large bar*
Time: *30 mins*

Ingredients:
50g raw cacao butter
3 tablespoons coconut sugar
1 teaspoon vanilla extract
50g raw cacao powder

Homemade chocolate makes a perfect gift. Family and friends will love you forever for it. Use organic cacao for the best nutritional opportunities and always buy fairly traded varieties to make sure that you are supporting ethical cacao practices.

Raw cacao is chock-full of antioxidants, healthy fats, protein, polyphenols, minerals and vitamins. The theobromine in cacao has been shown to help stimulate the central nervous system, whilst relaxing smooth muscles and dilating the blood vessels. Chemicals naturally present have also been found to encourage serotonin and other neurotransmitters that help inspire a good mood. Cacao contains various components like alkaloids, proteins, beta-carotene, leucine, linoleic, lipase, lysine, and theobromine, that all work together to improve physical and mental health. If you can't find the raw version, then you can also use cocoa (which is the roasted version), although seek out the highest quality, organic type possible.

1. Coconut sugar is usually coarse when purchased. Ideally, grind the coconut sugar down to a fine consistency using a nut mill/grinder or nutri-bullet. Otherwise, simply use it as is. However, a fine grain allows the sugar to dissipate evenly throughout the chocolate, ensuring that it does not sink to the bottom as the chocolate sets.
2. Cacao butter either comes in a solid block, as chunks or as buttons. If it is in a solid block or in chunks then shave or slice off the amount you need. Thin shaved slices allow the cacao butter to crumble. If you purchase the cacao butter as buttons, then use them as they are.
3. Get a saucepan and add about an inch of water. Place a heatproof glass bowl on top of or inside the pan and heat the water on the lowest setting.
4. Melt the cacao butter in the glass bowl (the minimum temperature for melting is 34°C). The watchword here is "melt", rather than "overheat". Add the coconut sugar and vanilla at this stage and mix regularly over the next few minutes. Note: if too much heat is applied, then it takes longer to cool and the mix will have a thin consistency. It also means that the coconut sugar is more likely to sink to the bottom of the chocolate when setting. The easiest way to prevent this is to finely grind the sugar as explained above.
5. When the cacao butter has melted, add the cacao powder and mix thoroughly. If you have overheated the contents, then take the bowl out of the water and let it cool down a little before carrying on.
6. Pour the mixture into a chocolate bar mould or a parchment paper lined container.
7. The quickest way to set the chocolate is in the freezer, but a fridge is fine .
8. Once the chocolate solidifies, pop it out of the mould or, if using a container, cut the chocolate slab with a knife or snap it. It's delicious. Enjoy!

Cooked Desserts

Makes: *8 slices*

Time: *55 mins*

The Kind Bakewell Tart

Bakewell tart is a popular English confection dating back to the 1800s. The traditional recipe essentially breaks down into three parts: (i) a short crust pastry base, (ii) jam filling and (iii) an almond-infused, sponge topping. I adored this dessert when I was growing up and was actually starting to miss it in my life. So the day I came up with a healthy, gluten-free, vegan version, made without refined sugar, I was completely overjoyed. All my British friends have gotten really excited about this, telling me how remarkably convincing it tastes. A little hint when making this: some of the ingredients in the different sections are similar, so don't forget which part you are doing mid-way through. (Voice of experience speaking here - I got totally distracted once and ended up getting in a real muddle with this one!)

Pastry Ingredients:

125g rice flour

75g tapioca flour (or tapioca starch)

4 tablespoons coconut oil

4 tablespoons rice syrup

1 teaspoon vanilla extract

Cake Topping Ingredients:

Dry topping ingredients

75g rice flour

75g tapioca flour

50g ground almonds

1 teaspoon bicarbonate of soda

1 heaped tablespoon ground flaxseeds

Wet topping ingredients

75ml rice syrup

75ml water

75ml coconut oil

1 teaspoon almond essence

1 teaspoon apple cider vinegar

Filling

A few heaped spoons of sugar-free spread

Make the pastry base first:

1. Lightly oil the tart dish (approximately 25cm or 10inch diameter) with a dash of coconut oil.
2. Briefly mix the rice flour, tapioca flour and ground flaxseeds together in a bowl.
3. Add the coconut oil (melt first, if solid), rice syrup and vanilla extract. Mix in with a spoon. Once it has started to combine together nicely, use the back of your spoon (or hands if it needs extra help to combine) to 'press' it all together until you have one large ball of pastry. If it's cold then definitely use your hands to combine. The warmth of your hands will soften the coconut oil and make it pliable.
4. It may be easier if you roll out your ball with a rolling pin a little first, although you don't need to roll it out all the way (as you would conventional pastry). Roll it out just enough to roughly cover slightly less than the bottom of the dish. Then, to line the whole dish (base and sides), press and push the dough evenly to spread it all the way up the sides. There is an art to doing this, involving pushing and pressing with both hands to spread across the bottom of the dish - somewhat like a massage therapist - and then using nimble fingers to push up the sides. With a little practice you'll get the hang of it. **Note:** if your kitchen is chilly then the pastry might be too brittle to roll out (it tends to break apart more when the coconut oil cools down). In which case, just use your hands to manually push and spread the dough over the whole dish and forget trying to roll it out with a rolling pin.
5. Once you've lined the dish, put it in the fridge and complete the rest of the recipe.

Make the cake topping:

1. Now would be a great time to preheat the oven to gas mark 4 (180°C/350°F) so that it will be ready and hot by the time you've done the topping.
2. Mix all the dry topping ingredients together in a mixing bowl.
3. Mix all the wet ingredients in a jug.
4. Pour the wet ingredients into the bowl and thoroughly mix in with the dry. You might get a bit of a 'fizz' as the vinegar reacts with the bicarbonate of soda .
5. Take the pastry-lined tart dish out of the fridge and put an even layer of sugar-free fruit spread or jam onto the base, using a few generous heaped dessertspoon's worth.
6. Pour the cake mixture into the pastry base. If the mixture rapidly turns thick (which often happens if your kitchen is a little chilly), just spoon it in and spread across the base. As soon as it heats in the oven, the cake mixture will distribute itself evenly for you. Pop it into the oven.
7. Bake on a medium to high shelf for approximately 35 minutes.
8. When ready, take out and place on a cooling rack and allow to cool completely before attempting to cut. The nature of gluten-free pastry means that it will likely crumble if you don't let it cool down first.

Oat Cookies - 3 Ways

These cookies are pleasingly moist on the inside, with a subtle crunch on the outside. Oats are naturally gluten-free, but if you are strictly avoiding gluten then please note that contamination can occur if the oats have been processed in a factory that also processes wheat, barley and rye. In which case, be sure to purchase certified gluten-free oats.

Coco-choc cookies

Makes: *14 cookies*
Time: *25 mins*

Ingredients:
200g oats
4 heaped tablespoons desiccated coconut
4 heaped tablespoons chocolate or carob chips
6 tablespoons ground pecans or almonds
2 teaspoons ground cinnamon
1 small ripe banana
2 teaspoons vanilla extract
8 tablespoons (120ml) coconut oil
4 tablespoons (60ml) maple syrup

1. Preheat oven to gas mark 5 (190°C/375°F).
2. Roughly mix the dry ingredients together in a mixing bowl.
3. Mash the banana and drop it into the mixture.
4. Add the wet ingredients then mix-and-mash the whole medley together with a fork, until everything is mixed in and the banana is evenly distributed throughout.
5. Lightly oil a baking tray with coconut oil.
6. Divide mixture and form by rolling into balls then flattening into cookie shapes.
7. Pop into the oven for approximately 15 minutes (or until lightly tanned all over).
8. Take cookies out of the oven. Use a spatula to carefully lift off the tray and place on a cooling rack. Allow to fully cool before serving.

Granola choc chip Cookies

Makes: *14 cookies*
Time: *25 mins*

Ingredients:

1 tablespoon chai seeds
3 tablespoons water
300g oats
75g desiccated coconut
75g chocolate chips
1 teaspoon grated nutmeg
2 tablespoons ground cinnamon
1 small ripe banana
100ml coconut oil
150ml apple juice concentrate (or alternative)
2 teaspoons almond essence

1. Mix the chia seeds with the water and stir, leaving for a few minutes to form a gel.
2. Make as per the coco-choc cookies, adding the chia gel with the other ingredients.

Nirvana nutmeg cookies

Makes: *14 cookies*
Time: *25 mins*

Ingredients:

200g oats
6 tablespoons ground almonds
6 tablespoons desiccated coconut
4 heaped tablespoons raisins
2 teaspoons ground cinnamon
1 teaspoon freshly grated nutmeg
1 small ripe banana
2 tablespoons tahini
6 tablespoons coconut oil
4 tablespoons maple syrup
2 teaspoon vanilla extract

1. Make as per the coco-choc cookies.

Angelicious Chocolate Dream Cake

Welcome to my light & airy, richly delicious, dreamy chocolate cake. One magical day, after a request for a chocolate cake with a nice thick cacao cream on it, this is what happened! It has been a favourite ever since.

The ingredients listed are ideal for making in a 500g/1lb loaf tin (18 x 10 x 8cm or 7 x 4 x 3inches approx). However, if you want to make a big round cake, then simply double the ingredients and divide between two round, parchment-lined baking tins (with pop-out bottoms) and cook for about 25 minutes (rather than the 30 minutes, as in the instructions for the loaf tin version). Use some of the extra topping mix to sandwich the rounds together. Be careful to let the cake fully cool before you lift it. The gluten-free nature of this makes it quite a fragile cake, so take special care. Placing it in the fridge before icing will also help to firm it up really well.

Preparation ahead of time:

Soak the 'topping' dates for 1 or 2 hours before blending the chocolate cream (unless they are really soft, like medjool dates, in which case no is soaking required).

Making the cake:

1. Preheat your oven to gas mark 5 (190°C/375°F).
2. Mash banana with a fork and mix together with all dry ingredients in a large mixing bowl.
3. If your coconut oil is solid, make sure that you melt it before mixing with all the other wet ingredients. It turns to liquid above 24°C (76°F), so place it on a warm window-sill, or near somewhere warm to begin the melting process. If it is in a glass bottle or jar, you can melt it in a pan with really hot water. Once melted, mix it with all other wet ingredients in a jug.
4. Mix dry and wet ingredients together, until thoroughly combined. When ready, it should resemble a thick batter.
5. Line a 1lb loaf tin with parchment paper (or line two 8" round tins if doubling the mixture - *see previous page*).
6. Ladle or pour cake batter into the parchment-lined tin and pop into your preheated oven. Bake for 30 minutes (or 25 minutes if using 2 round tins).
7. When baked, take out and place on a cooling tray (if you have one - if not just use a plate). Note: cooling trays are useful because they let the air get under to assist the cooling process and don't trap in the hot moisture as a solid surface would.

Whilst the cake is cooling prepare the topping:

1. Thoroughly drain your soaked dates, draining off as much water as possible.
2. Scoop out the avocado then add to dates, along with cacao powder and vanilla extract. Blend together in a small jug with a hand blender until creamy smooth. Place in the fridge ready for the cake to cool down.
3. When the cake is cool, use a knife to spread a thick layer of chocolate cream all over the top and sides. This is a wonderfully light gluten-free cake, so you will need to spread the cream with a gentle touch.
4. Sprinkle a little desiccated coconut on top .
5. You can store in the fridge for a few days, although it does go a little firmer when chilled. I prefer to serve it at room temperature for the ultimate soft, divine, cake texture.

Serves: *8*
Time: *60 mins*
(plus soak time)

Dry Ingredients:

1 medium-sized ripe banana
100g rice flour
25g tapioca flour
25g millet flour
50g cacao powder
1 teaspoon bicarbonate of soda

Wet Ingredients:

100ml maple syrup
100ml water
100ml coconut oil
1 teaspoon apple cider vinegar
1 teaspoon vanilla extract

Chocolate Dream Topping:

100g pitted dates
½ medium ripe avocado
1 heaped tablespoon cacao powder
1 teaspoon vanilla extract
Desiccated coconut to garnish

Fig-A-Licious Tart

Serves: *4 - 6*
Time: *50 mins*
(plus soak time)

Ingredients:

250g dried figs (plus water to soak)
*1 heaped teaspoon orange
(or lemon peel)*
75g brown rice flour
75g tapioca flour/starch
1 heaped tablespoon ground flaxseeds
3 tablespoons coconut oil
3 tablespoons brown rice syrup
1 teaspoon vanilla extract

I love dispelling the myth that healthy food can't be absolutely delicious. There's something really satisfying about eating a dessert that not only tastes scrumptious, but is also full of healthy ingredients. Like all of the recipes in this book, my 'Fig-a-licious Tart' is free from dairy, egg, wheat, gluten, refined sugar. Free from nasties and it STILL tastes delectable. We absolutely love this one here (and had fun naming it too!).

You need a round baking tin with a pop out bottom (20cm/8inches in diameter) or something similar. The pop out bottom isn't essential, although it will help you to get the tart out when it has baked.

1. Soak figs in water overnight (or at least 3 hours) to soften for blending.
2. Preheat the oven to gas mark 6 (200°C/400°F).
3. Finely grate orange peel (or lemon peel).
4. Drain figs and blend together with the grated orange peel. Put this to the side whilst you prepare the gluten-free pastry.
5. Briefly mix rice flour, tapioca flour and ground flaxseeds together in a mixing bowl.
6. Mix in coconut oil, rice syrup and vanilla essence with a spoon. Once it starts to combine together nicely, use the back of your spoon to press it all together until you have one large ball of pastry.
7. Lightly oil the cake tin.
8. Take about half of the pastry ball, place it in the middle of the tin and press downward in all directions until it is evenly spread all over. This should create a layer about ½cm (¼inch) thick. If it's a bit too thick in one place and lacking in another, just press and push (a bit like being a pastry massage therapist!) until it's sort of even. Doesn't have to be perfect.
9. Create a fig layer on top of the pastry by spreading your blended fig mixture evenly all over. Spoon it on and then spread with a blunt knife.
10. Take the remaining pastry from the mixing bowl and form into a thick cylindrical shape. Lightly flour your kitchen counter top and begin to roll until the pastry is approximately ¼cm thick. This can be a little fiddly, but gets much easier with practice.
11. Use a sharp knife to cut your rolled pastry into strips approximately 1cm (½inch) wide. Carefully lift strips (using a cake slice/spatula if you have one) and form a lattice pattern on top of the pie. There is a bit of an art to creating a lattice pattern and, honestly, the best way to learn is just to make it up as you go along. If you don't want to create a lattice then use your creativity to do whatever you feel like on top instead.
12. Bake for approximately 25 minutes or until the pastry begins to tan on top.
13. Serve warm, right away or allow to cool. The tart should keep nicely for a few days in a sealed container. (Beware though, it's one of those tasty delights that seems to mysterious disappear as soon as you turn your back!).

COCONUT RICE PUDDING
WITH HINTS OF
NUTMEG & CINNAMON

Serves: 4

Time: *45 mins*

Ingredients:

200g brown long-grain rice
50g raisins or chopped dates
Water (to cook rice with)
1 teaspoon freshly grated nutmeg
1 teaspoon ground cinnamon
Pinch ground cardamom
300ml full-fat canned coconut milk
2 tablespoons maple syrup
2 teaspoons vanilla extract
Extra rice milk (or coconut) to thin

Milky puddings were always my favourite desserts during childhood. I adored that nurturing, hearty feeling of my mam's oven-baked 'made-with-love' rice pudding. Many years later, I get to enjoy this alternative healthy version instead. With flavoursome hints of nutmeg and cinnamon, its rich, creamy coconut milk makes for an aromatic tropical experience. The rice and coconut are naturally sweet and with the addition of maple syrup, for extra eloquence, and dried fruit, to satisfy your sweet palate, you've got a deliciously balanced, good, healthy pudding.

1. Cook the rice and raisins in a pan with about 3 times as much water as the rice. The cooking time for the rice on its own should be about 30 minutes (or alternatively, 5 minutes less than the packet instructs). You don't need to fully cook the rice at this stage.
2. Once you've finished this first cooking stage, strain the rice and raisins then rinse through with water to get rid of any extra starch.
3. Allow water to drain off and place the rice and raisins back into the pan.
4. Add freshly grated nutmeg, ground cinnamon, ground cardamom, coconut milk, maple syrup and vanilla extract. Stir in and gently cook for a further 10 minutes or until the rice is fully cooked. Stir frequently.
5. If the pudding is too thick (or not creamy enough) at this stage add some rice milk or more coconut milk to thin and cream-up to desired consistency.
6. Serve hot or cold.

Banana & Almond Chocolate Magic Muffins

Makes: *6 big muffins*
Time: *30 mins*

Dry Ingredients:

1 large ripe banana

100g brown rice flour

50g ground almonds

1 heaped tablespoon of cocoa (or carob) powder

50g chocolate chips

1 teaspoon bicarbonate of soda

Wet Ingredients:

100ml coconut oil

75ml rice syrup

75ml rice milk

1 teaspoon apple cider vinegar

This is a tasty, delicately light, gluten-free, melt in the mouth muffin experience. Being gluten-free means that they don't tend to give you that 'OMG I am stuffed' feeling that comes with eating conventional cake. The alchemical blend of apple cider vinegar and bicarbonate of soda plays an important role, since it is responsible for the cake becoming all airy and light.

1. Preheat the oven to gas mark 6 (200°C/400°F).
2. Mash the banana in a mixing bowl.
3. Melt the coconut oil ready for pouring by leaving in a warm place ahead of time; or if your oil is in a glass bottle, melt by placing it in a pan of hot water.
4. Add the remaining dry ingredients to the mixing bowl along with the banana and mix together.
5. Whisk all the wet ingredients together with a fork.
6. Add the wet ingredients to the dry and mix thoroughly.
7. Evenly spoon the mixture into 6 muffin cases in a deep muffin tin.
8. Bake on the middle shelf of your preheated oven for approximately 20 minutes. The cakes should have risen a little and feel cooked on top. It's difficult to tell if they have tanned because they should look chocolatey brown anyway.
9. Allow them to cool in the muffin tin a little before handling. They will be delicate once cooked, so handle with care. Gently tilt and lift out of the cupcake tin then place on a cooling rack.

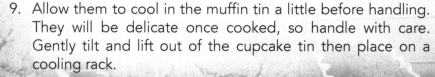

Creating food consciously is a celebration of compassion for all sentient life. Never doubt that you are making a difference. Positive change begins with one single act of love in the moment. Be a positive force for change.

Juicing For Health

Juicing For Optimal Health

There are few things in life as vibrant as fresh vegetable juice. It brings a rapid infusion of vitamins, minerals, antioxidants and phytonutrients into your body, whilst saving you the job of chomping your way through several salads' worth of veggies or fruits. Juicing offers you an excellent way of absorbing the abundance of nutritional content from vegetables into your body. The more nutrition that you assimilate, the better you are going to feel and the more you will rejuvenate, revitalise and nourish your beautiful self.

Juice is also one of the best forms of water available. Water is one of the body's most important requirements for a healthy, functioning system; although, rather unfortunately, it can be a little challenging to come by pure, clean water these days. If you are using organic fruits and vegetables (which I highly recommend) then your juice will contain one of the best sources of water available.

In this day and age, with pollutants and the stresses of life, we are really missing out on a special opportunity if we don't juice. It is a massive investment in your vitality and wellness. Once you start to bring it into your weekly rhythm, it's easy. You'll quickly begin to feel that alive, expanded feeling as your vibration rises.

Incredible taste
If you are new to juicing or you have only ever bought vegetable juice from a bottle on a supermarket shelf, then you'd be forgiven for being a little reserved about the taste of juice. I can't actually drink the stuff unless it's fresh. The truth is that homemade vegetable juices can be out-of-this-world delicious if you find a blend that works for you. I often add a little apple or pear into my juice to balance the flavours of vegetables and herbs. Not only can the taste be awesome, but they are bursting with so much energy that they even put coffee to shame! The secret is to give it a chance, to notice how it makes you feel inside and see how you really start to shine, and then make a choice.

Finding your own juicing rhythm
I've found that fresh vegetable juice is one of the best ways to start the day. It's like plugging into a cosmic power source and immediately has me feeling alive and set up for my busy schedule. Some people love to juice daily, whilst others have a set day every week. Other people like to do a juice cleanse over a few days every now and again. Embrace what works for you and find your own unique juicing rhythm, so that no matter what might come along to get in the way, you are going to enjoy the benefits of freshly pressed veggie juice. Once you get into the swing of it, they're actually quite quick to make. The good that it will do you far outweighs the small amount of effort that it takes. Your health is going to totally thank you for it.

"Let food be thy medicine and
medicine be thy food."
Hippocrates

WHICH JUICER?

There are different types of juicers; something for everyone. The most modern juicers are designed for super busy people, with minimal chopping and cleaning required. Good juicers squeeze most of the juice out, leaving behind only fibrous pulp.

Juicers come in all different shapes and sizes. Here's an outline of what options are out there:

CITRUS JUICER: most of us have access to a citrus juicer of some sort. They often come as the most basic type where you halve your citrus fruit, pressing it down and twisting on a cone-like part - which essentially separates the juice from the rest of the fruit. They also come in electrical versions and as food processor attachments. A citrus juicer is ideal if you regularly juice lots of oranges, grapefruit or lemons etc. Their limitation is that they don't juice a whole lot else.

CENTRIFUGAL JUICER: this is the most common type of juicer available, perhaps because it is generally priced low. The technology is designed to push hard veggies and fruits into a meshed chamber, where the flesh is rapidly separated from the juice. Centrifugal juicers are rather loud, don't tend to work so well with less juicy vegetables, like leafy greens, and also leave a lot of pulp. They are known to oxidise the juice more quickly than masticating juicers, and so the juice tends to lose the nutrients more quickly. They are however, a great place to start if you want to explore juicing for the first time without taking the full plunge, or if you juice lots of juicy fruits.

MASTICATING JUICERS: these juicers effectively chew vegetables and hard fruits for you, producing a high quality cold-pressed type juice. With a slower, more sophisticated action, they manage to squeeze much more of the juice out whilst working so much better with greens, wheatgrass and herbs than a centrifugal juicer. So as well as squeezing more juice out of your veggies, you can also benefit from more of the nutritional goodness from your vegetables and fruits with less waste. Whilst they aren't cheap, they are really good value for money (and let's face it, you are worth it!). I've owned a single-geared masticating juicer for the best part of 15 years now and it's served me incredibly well. There are essentially three types of masticating juicers...

MANUAL MASTICATING JUICER: this is an inexpensive masticating option with no electricity required. It gives you a great work-out and takes quite a bit longer than electrical models. However, it works perfectly well if you do have the extra time to turn the handle and do the grinding yourself. It's a much kinder way to juice your veggies and hard fruits - plus it's a great way of infusing your positive vibes into the produce.

SINGLE GEAR HORIZONTAL MASTICATING JUICER: to date this has been the most popular kind of juicer. They are usually much less expensive than the super serious twin gear professional triturating models. They are often easy to clean and are great at juicing greens and herbs as well as all other hard fruits and veggies.

VERTICAL SLOW MASTICATING JUICER: this is the newest kid on the block and has taken the juice world by storm. They are essentially a redesigned single gear masticating juicer, with a much larger screen to work the juice through. They are fast yet thorough. Designed for ease of use and optimal efficiency, they're pretty awesome. They tend to have a large funnel, so minimal (if any) chopping of fruits and veggies is required. They are easy to clean and have a reputation for squeezing optimal amounts of nutritional goodness out of your veggies and fruits.

TRITURATING JUICERS (TWIN GEARED): these are the ultimate juicers, producing a premium quality juice. They work in a similar way to the single geared masticating juicer, although with twin gears they work much harder to get the maximum benefit from the produce. They are the top contender when it comes to juicing wheatgrass, herbs and other greens. If you are healing from a major illness like cancer, then this would be your new best friend. They are the most expensive models to purchase, although they do unleash the maximum levels of phytonutrients and enzymes available. So if you are serious about juicing and can afford it, this would be the one for you.

Let's get juicing

The next section is dedicated to some of my favourite juice blends, all bursting with different health benefits. There isn't much else to say about how to juice, other than to always buy organic if possible. When you are ready, just chop your veggies to the size that fits through your juicer funnel, push them through with the plunger and watch it turn into nature's finest nectar.

Beetiful Mint Detox

1 large beetroot
1 small handful fresh mint
4 celery stalks
4 large kale leaves
2 pears

Dandelion & Apple Juice

Big handful young dandelion
greens
2 sweet apples
3 large celery stalks
2 kale leaves
½ cucumber

Rosemary Memory Juice

Handful fresh rosemary
1 teaspoon fresh ginger
4 big kale leaves
4 celery stalks
1 apple
1 lemon

Carrot & Ginger Zinger

5 medium carrots
5 celery stalks
1 large apple
1 teaspoon fresh ginger

Fennel Cleanse

1 large fennel bulb with leaves
2 apples
4 large celery stalks

Grapefruit Purifier

2 red or pink grapefruit
...that's all!

Green Warrior Tonic

A few thick celery stalks
Several really big kale leaves
2 medium-sized apples
Handful of fresh coriander leaves
Half a lemon (no peel)

Pure Focus Nectar

1 large beetroot
4 celery stalks
1 lemon (no peel)
1 teaspoon fresh ginger
1 large pear

Ginger Power Detox

1 small beetroot
8 celery stalks
3 carrots
1 heaped teaspoon fresh ginger
1 large apple

Wellness Wonder Juice

1 large beetroot
1 large carrot
2 medium apples
2 large kale leaves
1 lemon (no peel)

Measuring for International Readers

When I published my first book in 2013, I had no idea that well over half of my readers would be international! I am so deeply touched that people are happy to move beyond geographical boundaries to embrace the delights of conscious cuisine. Finding a way to unite us all is an exciting challenge. One main area that differs internationally with recipes, is the way we measure ingredients.

You will notice that this book uses the metric method of measuring. A lot of people will be familiar with this, using weighing scales, measuring spoons and metric jugs. However, if you don't already have these, it's well worth getting some. Having said that, quite a few of my recipes are forgiving if you stray from the original quantities. I've created these handy conversion charts to help if you are more familiar with 'cups' or 'ounces' instead. The most important thing is that you enjoy your adventures in the kitchen and have an awesome time!

Converting liquids

Liquid measurements are easy to convert because they have standard conversions as you can see on the right.

An Australian or Canadian cup is 250ml. A US cup is 240ml.

Ideally you'll have a measuring jug that lists ml or fluid oz for a more accurate conversion.

Note: *these charts involve a little rounding up to the nearest whole and sensible figure. A tiny little extra or little less, really shouldn't make much difference on most recipes.*

Liquid measurements			
Metric	**US Imperial**	**Canadian/Australian cups**	**US Cups**
25ml	1fl oz		
60ml	2fl oz	¼ cup	¼ cup
75ml	2½fl oz	⅓ cup	⅓ cup
100ml	3½fl oz		
125ml	4¼ fl oz	½ cup	½ cup
150ml	5fl oz	⅔cup	⅔cup
175ml	6fl oz	¾ cup	¾ cup
200ml	6¾fl oz		
250ml	8½fl oz	1 cup	1 cup
300ml	10fl oz/½ pint	1 ⅓ cup	1¼ cups
350ml	12fl oz	1 ½ cups	1 ½ cups
400ml	13½fl oz	1 ¾ cups	1 ¾ cups
450ml	15fl oz	2 cups	2 cups
473ml	16fl oz (1 US pt)	2 cups	2 cups
500ml	17fl oz		
750ml	25fl oz	3⅓ cups	
1 litre	40fl oz	4⅓ cups	4¼ cups

Converting dry ingredients

You can get a fairly accurate conversion by using imperial weighing scales to convert as follows...

Converting from grammes to cups can be a bit more iffy. Some recipes really don't mind a bit of variation. Creating recipes offers the perfect opportunity to embrace your intuition and feel what's right.

Grammes to ounces	
Metric	**US Imperial**
15g	½ oz
20g	¾ oz
30g	1 oz
40g	1½oz
50g	1¾oz
60g	2oz
75g	2½oz
100g	3½oz
125g	4oz
140g	4½oz
150g	5 ⅓oz
175g	6oz
200g	7oz
225g	8oz
250g	9oz
275g	10oz
300g	11oz
350g	12oz
375g	13oz
400g	14oz
425g	15oz
450g	16oz (1lb)
500g	18oz
750g	1lb 11oz
1kg	2¼lb

Ingredients in grammes to cups		
Ingredient	**1 cup**	**½ cup**
Raisins	200g	100g
Oats	90g	45g
Oatmeal	100g	50g
Rice flour	120g	60g
Nuts	150g	75g
Nuts/seeds (ground)	120g	60g
Syrup	320g	160g
Chocolate chips	150g	75g
Cocoa powder	120g	60g
Desiccated coconut	70g	35g
Tapioca flour	110g	55g
Rice	180g	90g
Buckwheat flakes	100g	50g

CPSIA information can be obtained
at www.ICGtesting.com
Printed in the USA
BVHW021750040920
588148BV00001B/1